Praise for *SuperLoop*

An inspiring and practical system for operating conscious businesses while being a conscious leader.

—DR. DEEPAK CHOPRA, MD

Author, *The Seven Spiritual Laws of Success, Quantum Healing,* and others

In her new book, *SuperLoop*, highly acclaimed social entrepreneur Susan Leger Ferraro offers a radical idea—the creation of a "human" model of the workplace— a place that celebrates feelings and beliefs in a conscious way to build successful business cultures. Beautifully written, *SuperLoop* offers the "how to" for businesses that want to keep their employees and to reclaim humanity while still meeting the bottom line.

—KATHY HIRSH-PASEK

Professor of psychology, Temple University; author, *Einstein Never Used Flashcards* and *Becoming Brilliant*

SLF is a visionary whose enthusiasm for the world she imagines is contagious.

Leger Ferraro is a leader who walks the walk, sharing brilliance and insight gleaned from four decades of experience—from the seventeen-year-old entrepreneur to the wildly successful creator, mother, grandmother and CEO of six multi-million-dollar businesses.

Read *SuperLoop* to be inspired, challenged, and guided—by a guide of the highest integrity, skill, and wisdom—to make a better world for yourself, your colleagues and all those you love. It is possible to create successful businesses where people thrive. Leger Ferraro leads the way.

—SARA SCHLEY

CEO, Seed Systems; co-founder, B Corp B The Change Women CEOs; author, *BrainStorm;* filmmaker, *BrainStorm*

Kudos to Susan Leger Ferraro for penning a timely and masterful book.

The two pillars of success are having grit and being happy.

The author drawing from her vast experience and her profound insights and visionary leadership has gifted us this remarkable book.

Read it, and incorporate the many lessons learned and it will certainly foster transformative change in any business endeavor.

This is a must read for any organization that wants to lead with both mind and heart.

—SANJIV CHOPRA, MBBS, MACP

Professor of medicine, Harvard Medical School

I'm honored and proud to have the opportunity to share my thoughts on Susan Leger Ferraro's phenomenal body of work, *SuperLoop*. I'm an Operational Excellence pro, lean six sigma master black belt, performance coach, and mergers and acquisitions advisor who's been equally dedicated to integrating community service, localized economic development, and cultivating learning, education, and uplift within all of our business engagements and project deployments. I thought we were really on to something … Then I started reading Susan's masterpiece!

My mantra has always been, "Everything Counts" and I'm very confident in proclaiming that *SuperLoop* will more than adequately prepare the reader with a very organized, relatable construct that heightens understanding, situational awareness and sincere human emotion. If you're also an advocate of "success is always in the details," you'll be enthused to know that Susan has provided a comprehensive guide of successful strategies and tactics to responsibly empower conscious leadership, cultivating thriving humancentric systems and endorsing the DNA of being good humans who want to change the world for the betterment of everyone. I'm now relentlessly pursuing becoming a SuperLoop Praxis practitioner … and an even better contributor to humanity!

—JOHN HOWARD II

Founder and CEO, JH2 Performance Group, LLC

I've waited more than a decade for this treasure of a book by Susan Leger Ferraro! The rewards are renewed employee engagement coupled with increased company performance through time-tested, proven processes which Susan labels as "Actionable Awareness." These processes serve to leverage humanity from a base of authenticity. Here's the guide to a better way of working and living!

—JACK DALY

CEO, coach, and serial entrepreneur

This powerful, inspiring book embodies a refreshing humanistic approach, reminding us that behind every business strategy and decision lies the heartbeat of humanity. With profound insight and empathy, Susan champions the idea that success isn't just about numbers, but also about uplifting individuals and communities. Through her writing, Susan inspires us to lead with compassion, empathy, and a deep understanding of the human experience, creating a brighter, more fulfilling future for all. This book is a "game changer" for any organization.

—GARY McGUEY

Senior lead consultant and coach; author, *Mentor in Me* and
The Inspirational Teacher

I've seen many of the challenges Susan mentions in *SuperLoop*, at companies large and small, including Microsoft and Google.

Beliefs, biology, and behavior are key factors in optimal performance. It is about alignment when creating a passionate team committed to the mission. Believing in that mission and trusting the team to do their part are the foundations of high-functioning teams. If work is a collection of never-ending tasks, that isn't a mission. Individual contributors completing work assignments alone aren't a team. It is surprising how many companies fail to articulate their mission, and each team member's part in it. *SuperLoop* is about designing a comprehensive model to connect mission and passion to the people who create results in our organizations and the world.

—DON DODGE

VP, Google, Microsoft, Napster

As an author who has spent over thirty years in the publishing industry, with more than five hundred books published, but above all as an avid reader and editor, I must say that *SuperLoop: How Understanding Our Beliefs, Biology, and Behavior Can Create a Business That Works for Every ONE* by Susan Leger Ferraro goes beyond the conventional proposals of empowerment and entrepreneurship books. She validates every word with her own experience, and I can attest to that because I know that everything she touches turns not only into gold, but a world of prosperity and happiness. She showcases the brightest side of a productive society where humans are always the most important value—the protagonist and beneficiary of progress.

Reading this book has been nothing short of a revelation. It's not just insightful —it's transformative!

From the outset, Susan's words struck a chord within me. She deftly articulates the discord that exists in our workplaces today, a dissonance that I, and many others, have wrestled with. But more than just identifying the problem, Susan provides a road map for change.

Wise woman for whom problems are only the seed of a fruitful solution!

SuperLoop stands out for its commitment to practical, actionable change. Through the SuperLoop Praxis, Susan equips us with the tools and strategies to bring about meaningful transformation in our workplaces. She empowers us to create environments that are not just productive, but also deeply satisfying.

As I journeyed through the pages of *SuperLoop*, I found myself challenged, inspired, and ultimately, transformed. Susan's words are more than just a call to action—they are an invitation to embrace our shared humanity, to acknowledge the inherent worth of every individual, and to create spaces where everyone can thrive and flourish.

SuperLoop is more than a book—it's a manifesto for a new way of working, a testament to the power of empathy, compassion, and conscious leadership. It's a reminder that we all have the power to shape our reality, to create a world where work is not just a means to an end, but a source of joy, fulfillment, and meaning.

—YANITZIA CANETTI

CEO, Cambridge BrickHouse; author; professor

SuperLoop explains in a straightforward and very accessible way how to transform any organization into a more humane, effective, and sustainable system—simultaneously enhancing financial success and increasing social impact. Leveraging the latest scientific research on human flourishing, as well as Susan Leger Ferraro's own remarkable experience as entrepreneur, this engaging and inspiring book serves as an operating manual for success in an era of conscious capitalism.

—PHIL ZELAZO, PHD

Nancy M. and John E. Lindahl professor, University of Minnesota; co-founder, Reflective Performance, Inc.

Susan has always been a visionary in how to connect the pillars of humanity, civic engagement, and purposeful entrepreneurship. In *SuperLoop*, she brings all of that experience to the forefront, providing organizational leaders with a new understanding regarding how our individual beliefs, biology, and behavior impact workplace effectiveness and morale. Susan's insightful new approaches and perspectives enable leaders to create dynamic, humancentric work cultures that support and engage today's workforce, enabling their organizations to be more successful, productive, and equitable.

—KYLE ZIMMER

President, CEO, and co-founder, First Book

Susan Leger Ferraro is a thinker like no other. She has shown the capacity and drive to work across domains as disparate as early education, beauty, food and employment post-recidivism. From this body of work, she has extracted a set of leadership best practices that, frankly, the rest of all would be hard pressed to determine. Thankfully, she has now put pen to paper, and the result is *SuperLoop*. If you want to push your thinking about leadership to a whole new level, I cannot recommend this book more highly.

—FRANCES K. HURLEY, EdD

Principal, Hurley International

An approachable and interesting read, *SuperLoop* is informative, authentic and practical. Susan walks the walk, offering a master class in implementing business practices for a human-centered and more sustainable future.

—MARY HAGGERTY

Director of Media Engagement, GBH

SuperLoop offers a framework for working with people to get the results we want for others by creating conditions that allow for curiosity and appreciation of the individuals doing the work. The book offers practical tools, actionable suggestions, and tools for individuals and organizations that lead to transformation through conscious choices. Conscious choices are a crucial driver in tailoring our actions to listen to and respond to young children, families, and communities historically marginalized by existing programs, policies, practices, and institutions.

—SHERRI KILLINS STEWART, EdD

President/CEO, Leaders Making It Possible, Inc.

SuperLoop, like Susan herself, dares to center humanity in running a successful business. As traditional extractive business cultures crumble, here rises *SuperLoop*: both an invitation and set of practices that call us to take care of one another as we take care of business. Spoiler alert: the practices here will up-level not only how you do business, but the quality of your relationships, in and outside of work. If ever there was a moment for a road map of human-centered, time-tested, whole-human business practices, it is now. Welcome to *SuperLoop*, where consciousness meets sustainable business. What a gift!

—CHRISTINE ZANCHI, EdM, CPCC

Start-up advisor, R&D executive, and executive coach

Susan Leger Ferraro teaches us the art of transformation: for ourselves, our work-places, and communities, and in doing so, the world. A champion of inclusive and equitable workplaces, Leger Ferraro promotes a vision of how we can build workplaces and communities that work for all and allow us to call each other forward. From her work as an entrepreneur, advisor to companies, educator, and coach, Susan brings her wisdom, science, expertise, and neuroscience to the rescue. This book will help you to build human centric organizations which promote the "I" and elevate the "we" and the "all." We start now.

—DEBORAH LEIPZIGER

Author, *The Corporate Responsibility Code Book*; founder, the Lexicon of Change

SuperLoop is being sold as a business book, for good reason, but it's so much more than that. The core of the principles and ideas throughout it is our connected humanness, compassion and personal and interpersonal flourishing. So, maybe it's fair to say that it's a business book with a soul and a heart (thank God!).

Ms. Leger Ferraro has given us a template, not just for how to run our organi-zations, but how to live a more authentic and empathetic life in general. And how when we do this our places of work, our organizations, and even our personal lives and relationships all improve.

And we shouldn't be surprised by this take, as the author is the walking embodiment of advocating for authenticity, realness and shared human experiences.

In a time when our world seems so disconnected and the workplace feels the same, the author gives a blueprint for how to come together and create more harmony, empathy, and results through authentic communication and connec-tion. One of the focuses of *SuperLoop* is supporting a "more human model work culture—and that this more human-centered work model could make organiza-tions more effective." I would take it further and suggest that a more human-centered LIFE model is needed now more than ever. And knowing the author as I do, she is suggesting the same thing.

I have been on the receiving end of her coaching and trainings for many years, and I have walked away not only armed with practical skills and tangible take-aways, but I have walked away a better, more compassionate, loving and equity-based leader. More importantly I've walked away a better person.

Ms. Leger Ferraro states, "There is no actual divide between our work lives and the rest of our lives." She makes the point that by creating BETTER people in the work environment they go on to be BETTER people in whole, out in the world. And I cannot think of a better mission as a great leader.

SuperLoop is a must read for not just business owners, executives and HR employees, but for all humans in any leadership or management positions wanting a more authentic, fulfilled life experience.

Kudos to *SuperLoop* for putting love and compassion back in the C-suite!

—MICHELLE ROSE GILMAN

Founder, Fusion Academy

Reading *SuperLoop: How Understanding Beliefs, Biology, and Behavior Can Build a Business That Works for Every ONE* I was immediately struck by the profound relevance and resonance of its themes—not just for the global community, but particularly for us in South Africa, where the struggle against generational poverty is a pressing reality.

Leger Ferraro masterfully intertwines the concepts of conscious education and ethical business operations, presenting a compelling case for their importance in empowering artists and driving socio-economic transformation. As a business educator, I found the exploration of these concepts both enlightening and invigorating.

The book's focus on elevating artists globally is particularly inspiring. By highlighting the immense, often untapped potential of artists, and proposing innovative strategies for their upliftment, the author provides a refreshing perspective on how we can harness creativity and talent to effect positive change. This vision is not only applicable to the arts sector but can also inspire broader initiatives aimed at poverty alleviation and wealth creation.

The author's proposed shift from generational poverty to generational wealth is a powerful call to action. The strategies and examples provided offer practical tools as to how this shift can be achieved, making it a valuable resource for educators, policymakers, business leaders, and artists alike.

SuperLoop is a must read, filled with innovative ideas, practical strategies, and inspiring stories. It is a guidebook for all of us striving to create a more equitable, prosperous, and artistically vibrant world.

—KHETI NGWENYA

Founder/CEO, SchoolMedia South Africa

As a musical artist and producer who has seen the transformative power of creativity firsthand, I found *SuperLoop: How Understanding Beliefs, Biology, and Behavior Can Create a Business That Works for Every ONE* to be a compelling and insightful read.

The author brilliantly bridges the worlds of business, biology, and behavioral science, presenting a unique approach that emphasizes the importance of understanding our beliefs and how they shape our perceptions and actions. The concept of the *SuperLoop* is a powerful tool for individuals and organizations alike, offering a new perspective to creating businesses that are not just profitable, but also equitable and socially conscious.

What resonated most with me was the book's focus on elevating the roles of artists and teachers. The author recognizes their critical contribution to society and the economy, and provides concrete strategies for how they can be empowered to help transform poverty into wealth. As an artist myself, this vision is both inspiring and empowering.

SuperLoop is a must read for anyone interested in creating sustainable change, whether in the business world, the arts, or education. It offers a powerful blueprint for building a business that truly works for everyone, and I believe it has the potential to inspire a new wave of conscious, inclusive entrepreneurship.

—GEMINI MAJOR

Malawian artist and producer

SuperLoop is an enlightening and transformative read centered around accountability and ethical leadership. This book delves deep into the principles of human-centric practices, emphasizing the importance of integrity, transparency, and social responsibility in today's world. SLF's insightful perspectives on how businesses can align profit with purpose inspire us to advocate for, and ourselves practice, whole human practices within the political landscape, fostering a culture of integrity and accountability at all levels of governance. I highly recommend *SuperLoop* to anyone seeking to create positive change in the world. This book is a powerful guide for building a more sustainable and ethical environment, and I am confident that its message will inspire meaningful and positive transformation in both corporate and political arenas.

—DIANA DIZOGLIO

Massachusetts state auditor

Superloop is far more than a book; it is a philosophy that embodies the principles of strong leadership.

Having had the privilege of working personally with Susan Leger Ferraro, I can strongly testify to the fact that this philosophy is rooted in decades of experience which has resulted in a magnitude of impact around the world.

Susan is living proof that you can marry commercial success with sustainable impact if the right approach is applied and *Superloop* is the guide to doing this.

Being someone who regularly works with creatives, I love how the book provides clear pathways to empower people to turn generational poverty into generational wealth.

I strongly recommend this book to anyone who wants to become a more holistic leader and people who, like myself, struggled with the balance between commercial success and impact.

—EASHAN THAKRAR

Founder, The Youth Project; founder/CEO, Mapogo Studios; co-founder, Imaginal Music

In *SuperLoop*, Susan Leger Ferraro demonstrates the truth to the saying that the important things we need in life, we learn in kindergarten. The founder of the academically and financially successful early childhood program, Little Sprouts, and a longtime leader in mindfulness and wellness programs, entrepreneur Leger-Ferraro has been bringing this knowledge to advise businesses like Verizon and The Body Shop and now shares her wisdom about how to create humane workplaces that work for employees and for the bottom line. In this book, you'll find truly innovative practices (such as replacing feedback with Feedforward) that will make you wish that this knowledge was much more widespread. Now it will be, thanks to *SuperLoop*!

—ELLEN GALINSKY

President, Families and Work Institute; best-selling author, *Mind in the Making* and *The Breakthrough Years*

SUPERLOOP

SUSAN LEGER FERRARO

SUPERLOOP

HOW UNDERSTANDING BELIEFS, BIOLOGY, AND BEHAVIOR
CREATES A BUSINESS THAT WORKS FOR EVERY ONE

Advantage | Books

Published by Advantage Books, Charleston, South Carolina.
An imprint of Advantage Media.

ADVANTAGE is a registered trademark, and the Advantage colophon is a trademark of Advantage Media Group, Inc.

Printed in the United States of America.

10 9 8 7 6 5 4 3 2 1

ISBN: 979-8-89188-218-8 (Hardcover)
ISBN: 978-1-64225-821-9 (Paperback)
ISBN: 978-1-64225-820-2 (eBook)

Library of Congress Control Number: 2024916643

Cover design by Matthew Morse.
Layout design by Megan Elger.

This publication is designed to provide accurate and authoritative information in regard to the subject matter covered. It is sold with the understanding that the publisher is not engaged in rendering legal, accounting, or other professional services. If legal advice or other expert assistance is required, the services of a competent professional person should be sought.

Advantage Books is an imprint of Advantage Media Group. Advantage Media helps busy entrepreneurs, CEOs, and leaders write and publish a book to grow their business and become the authority in their field. Advantage authors comprise an exclusive community of industry professionals, idea-makers, and thought leaders. For more information go to **advantagemedia.com**.

To my mom and dad for telling us they loved us, accompanied by a kiss good night—while teaching us the Golden Rule is the way to be a good human.

To my three sons who grew up with me and celebrated all the shenanigans throughout our lives. You are my best teachers.

To Maya Angelou for showing us all that defying societal rules to live your own principles may be the greatest act of courage we get to share.

CONTENTS

FOREWORD

SuperLoop: How Understanding, Beliefs, Biology, and Behavior Can Create a Business That Works for Every ONE offers groundbreaking insights into operationalizing consciousness and fostering healing cultures within organizations. At its core is the profound realization that perception shapes reality. By recognizing the power of beliefs to impact biology and behavior, we can shift mindsets toward empathy and inclusion.

Conscious leadership invites us to evolve our thinking and embrace how the past shapes the present. Processing emotions is critical to healing and growth. As I explored in my book *Awaken: A Journey to Purpose, Wholeness, and Healing*, uniting life's polarities connects us to innocence and healing. Leaders must prioritize their own emotional well-being and nurture authentic, vulnerable cultures of trust and support.

In 2016, Susan and I reconnected in our journeys as humans and leaders, sparking our passion to launch the first Conscious Capitalism gathering in Havana. There I witnessed Susan's conviction in action—integrating Conscious Capitalism with systems to organize healing communities, elevate potential, invest in leaders, and empower the marginalized to contribute.

SuperLoop underscores how conscious leadership unlocks human potential and cultivates lifelong learning. Leadership transcends profits—it's about imbuing work with purpose and meaning. A humancentric approach fosters empathy, resilience and empowerment for a sustainable, equitable future.

Drawing on Susan's forty-five-plus years as an executive and practitioner, the book offers accessible case studies from The Body Shop, The Chopra Center, and more, demonstrating how to manifest the ethos of "work is love made manifest." Through science-based practices, it shows how to maximize results for people, purpose, profit and planet.

May *SuperLoop* ignite consciousness, compassion and playful innocence in each reader, empowering them as agents of positive change. Together, let us awaken our true potential and co-create a future where business and humanity flourish as one. We can be good humans and run good businesses for a more just, integrated world.

RAJ SISODIA

Co-founder and former chairman, Conscious Capitalism Inc.
FEMSA Distinguished University Professor of Conscious Enterprise, Tecnológico de Monterrey

WE BEGIN WITH THE END

Y ou could say that the current era of my work to bring conscious principles and transformation to businesses began way back in 1996 in a huge glass and steel tower on Federal Street in downtown Boston. I was there on behalf of Verizon, which was interested in having me act as an expert consultant for their women's affinity group. I was there to teach a large group of C-suite leaders about Operationalizing Consciousness—about how to bring the ideas of mindfulness and self-awareness to their business in a way that would impact the day-to-day nature of their work in a measurable, tangible way. I was there to teach them about being more aware of themselves, their environment, and how they interacted with others—and how even their own identities and bodies

> **Operationalizing Consciousness is bringing the ideas of mindfulness and self-awareness to a business in a way that impacts the day-to-day nature of work in a measurable, tangible way.**

affect these interactions. I was there to center the idea of being good humans while running a good business that maximized performance outcomes for teams.

I was wearing a designer outfit that had cost me dearly. I'd purchased it at a consignment shop so that I looked professional for such an important meeting. My heart was in my throat. I'd never been in such an auspicious boardroom, let alone one filled with women who were focused solely on me and my ideas. I could feel the weight of their expectations and the weight of the responsibility I had in front of me. Doing well in this room would not only make my life better, but it would improve the lives of everyone there and all those they led.

I was a young single mother who had begun her business life with a series of early childhood enrichment centers that I'd founded when I was just out of high school in 1982 and had, using those schools as the foundation of my practice, developed a way to Operationalize the principles of a conscious life into the day-to-day work of a business. I was here to share my story with these executives and teach them how they could learn from what I'd done in terms of leadership, innovation, and creating world-class results.

As this group began to discuss the culture at Verizon, I remember being stunned at how effective and skilled the women of WAVE (Women's Association of Verizon Employees) were in their leadership roles. WAVE was an employee resource group built around breaking barriers, shattering glass ceilings, and cultivating advancement for the people within Verizon. The women in this group were truly impressive. Their ability to manage multimillion-dollar budgets and lead very large teams to victory in huge endeavors was absolutely stunning to me. Yet despite their internal mentorship, the progress that they'd made as individuals, and the fact that this room was filled with talent, this very successful group of women was dealing with the issues most (really all) companies deal with at some point: burnout, interpersonal conflict, leadership struggles, the absence of accountability, and the Artificial Harmony that encourages everyone not to acknowledge the issues around them. These problems were as constant in the 1990s as they are today. They've, in fact, really only gotten worse in the past thirty-five years.

That's because, ultimately, consciousness and humanity have been neglected as the important forces they are within a business, and we are now reaping the whirlwind of that neglect. We've tried to downplay the role of being human inside our organizations—despite the fact that our humanity is what makes our organizations strong. That dilemma has alienated people across our businesses.

We've hit a period where satisfaction in the workplace is at an all-time low. In the wake of the COVID-19 pandemic and large shifts in how people view work, we are in a place where we need to change the way that we approach the work environment. The dissatisfaction I've seen in my practice, which takes me across the length and breadth of global corporations, is staggering. Nearly six in ten employees were "quiet quitting" in a Gallup study of employees in 2022, and more than half of employees are actively looking for other work opportunities.[1] In 2024, these trends only seem to be accelerating, with only 30 percent of employees being highly engaged—the lowest reported numbers in twenty-one years.[2] We now see an increasing number of strikes, the Great Resignation, and even rising suicide rates.

We are facing an era where "deaths of despair," a term coined by Princeton sociologists Anne Case and Angus Deaton, are at an

---

1   "State of the Global Workplace: 2023 Report," Gallup, accessed June 6, 2024, https://www.gallup.com/workplace/349484/state-of-the-global-workplace-2023-report.aspx.

2   Jim Harter, "Employee Engagement Hits an 11-Year Low," Gallup, April 23, 2024, https://www.gallup.com/workplace/643286/engagement-hits-11-year-low.aspx.

all-time high.[3] The excess mortality from some combination of suicide, addiction, and alcohol-related diseases has generally climbed for Americans of virtually all demographics since the 1990s—and has elevated even more sharply since the 2020s and the COVID-19 pandemic.[4,5] There are profound consequences for not meeting human needs, and workers have progressively been feeling those consequences more and more deeply.[6]

On the executive side of the fence, it feels like I constantly hear that "people are unwilling to work anymore" and that companies "just can't find good talent." Some of those who are in positions of leadership don't seem to understand the increases in the cost of living or inflation; many don't understand that some work doesn't even pay enough for some workers to live. Even those who understand may not always show up to their teams in ways that indicate their empathy. The reality is that no amount of skimping, saving, or sacrifice can allow for some jobs to provide a livable lifestyle with our current attitudes toward work.

Nobody seems to have a good solution to these issues—and that's because they're unconsciously repeating the cycles that have led to these problems in the first place. On the organizational level, we consistently appeal to what hasn't worked. On the individual level, we operate on a pattern of reacting rather than responding, a cycle

---

3   Anne Case and Angus Deaton, *Deaths of Despair and the Future of Capitalism* (Princeton University Press, 2020).

4   Casey Mulligan, "Deaths of Despair and the Incidence of Excess Mortality in 2020," *VoxEU*, January 28, 2021, https://cepr.org/voxeu/columns/deaths-despair-and-incidence-excess-mortality-2020.

5   Jeffrey A. Bridge et al., "Youth Suicide during the First Year of the COVID-19 Pandemic," *Pediatrics* 151, no. 3 (2023), https://doi.org/10.1542/peds.2022-058375.

6   Hania Rahimi-Ardabili et al., "Have Deaths of Despair Risen during the COVID-19 Pandemic? A Systematic Review," *International Journal of Environmental Research and Public Health* 19, no. 19 (2022): 12835, https://doi.org/10.3390/ijerph191912835.

that then leads to a self-reinforcing feedback cycle known as "the SuperLoop."

The SuperLoop refers to the biological, behavioral, and belief systems that we use to navigate the world. The SuperLoop is based on what we have come to believe about the world, the biological reactions we have to situations (what gives us pleasure or pain, physical satisfaction or anxiety, dopamine or adrenaline), and what behaviors we use to respond to our bodies and beliefs. These situations often result in being trapped in patterns of anxiety and reaction that have become a dysfunction that starts on the individual level and then spreads up through the entire organization.

So what's wrong with our people? Our organizations? What can we do?

Enter SuperLoop Praxis, a practical, process-based means of engaging with the SuperLoop system to improve our happiness, responsibility, productivity, and ability to utilize our awareness and executive function. Best of all, SuperLoop Praxis scales from the individual to the team and then all the way up to the entirety of an organization. A group of committed humans working together and free from the ego, anxiety, and fear of their beliefs, biology, and behavior is a powerful force. This is a tangible path to unlocking human potential and maximizing performance—it's a path to making work an energizing force.

People want to work—they don't want to toil in an unfair environment where their humanity is denied or their work seems pointless. The founders of the United States of America risked their lives to have the freedom to choose their own path in life (including their professions). Dr. Martin Luther King's historic "I Have a Dream" speech was written for the 1963 March on Washington for **Jobs and Freedom**. Most of us forget the purpose of that moment and forget the fact that work and opportunity are a core part of how we live and find our freedom. The desire to do good work is integrated into our humanity.

We have a historic opportunity to collectively cocreate a system led by people who understand how to make work into a nurturing and effective force in our lives. If we seize it, we get to ignite a passion that changes everything, we get to provide the education that is a great equalizer, and we get to acknowledge that our relationship with ourselves radiates outward and touches everything and everyone around us.

But workers are only one side of the coin. Leaders want their companies and employees to succeed. No executive wants to intentionally run their company into the ground or to torture their workforce. They want to maximize results for the organizations they are committed to serving while also carrying out the passions that led them to leadership.

The fact is that both of these groups (both employers and employees) want what is best for their organizations and want to make meaningful contributions to the world. That means that the blame doesn't sit solely on the shoulders of any individual person. The problems we're facing across every industry stem from the increasingly toxic and negative cycles the global corporate system has normalized for itself by acting out top-down, command-and-control, zero-sum policies that don't live up to the universal implied social and material agreements between employers and employees.

When we sign on to work, we agree to show up and achieve results. When we are an employer, we are agreeing to provide an environment where those results are possible and where growth and change are not only allowed but are encouraged and cultivated. Right now, this agreement, for a multitude of reasons, has fallen by the wayside for many organizations.

The people in these organizations—both workers and leaders—are not satisfied with this version of the workplace, and the system is not set up to address this. We need a radical shift in consciousness—and we need to make that shift a reality within the structure of our behavior—to Operationalize it as a *Praxis*.

In my performance coaching, I consistently hear that people are "aware" of their blind spots and shortcomings. "My partner tells me that all the time." The next evolution of our own humanity is to recognize that there is more mental and emotional anguish from being aware of our shortcomings but not aligning it with changes in our behaviors. If we have awareness and we don't act, we suffer.

To paraphrase the apocryphal quote from philosopher Johann Goethe, "To know and not to do is not to know."[7]

This book is a culmination of everything I've worked on and through in my career. It's a guide to stepping toward what I call Actionable Awareness, which is the ability to be aware of the truth in ourselves and our environment and to act on that truth—this is the SuperLoop Praxis.

And it can change everything if we practice it.

That's a tall order and a big claim. So who am I to make it? Who was this woman making her pitch to a Verizon boardroom?

●   ●   ●

My name is Susan Leger Ferraro. I am the single parent of three men and Gigi to six grandkids. I'm the founder and CEO of six

---

7   This quote is popularly attributed to the writer and philosopher Goethe, who was frequently concerned with the gap between thought and practice. The true origin of the quote is unclear but is likely derived from Wilhelm Meister's *Wanderjahre* (*Apprenticeship*), book VII, chapter IX: "To act is easy, to think is hard; to act according to our thought is troublesome."

multimillion-dollar ventures. I have been an executive, consultant, and education expert for more than forty years. I began my career as a teenager (truly, a seventeen-year-old) when I opened a licensed family childcare center in a duplex I rented for $750 a month. I was so young that I would often walk up the street from my rented apartment to sleep at my parents' house, as I was afraid to sleep alone. Despite my young age, I had a clear mission in my work, and it was something that consumed my thoughts and stoked my passion for impacting the world almost every waking moment.

School had a mixed set of associations for me when I started Little Sprouts schools. I remember loving elementary school. I was a smart, outgoing child who loved to get attention for my intellect. As much as I craved the individual attention and praise from my teachers, however, I was confused by the fact that the boys in my classes attracted quite a bit of negative attention—they were constantly disciplined for being too noisy, for not fitting the educational mold as expected; often for what seemed like trivial breaches. When I first opened Little Sprouts, I wanted to do something that would create an environment where the many varieties of the way we are human were supported. It worked. I was improving the lives of both my students and my employees in a tangible way.

I was attracting the best people I could find and learning how to build a support network for them that could build their skills and competencies with education and organizational development. Together, we engaged in a system-supported form of learning that drew upon our collective strengths called "socialized learning." After I'd engineered the socialized learning environment, I created a small network of schools that tested at the top of our field, attracting the attention of both educators and professionals in outside organizations. We gradually garnered funding and support from institutions that were committed to innovative educational practices and achieving award-winning outcomes.

So then I opened another school. And then another. That network grew until there was a string of schools operating very successfully, even in places that faced the biggest challenges and obstacles from systemic racism and economic exclusion. Our school's test scores, literacy outcomes, and other metrics were extremely high because of the novel strategies that we employed at those schools, investing in human potential to maximize organizational performance.

My Little Sprouts schools were novel because we upended many of the corporate structures and attitudes that are taken for granted as defaults. Our organization changed the way we perceived work, employees, and leadership. At Little Sprouts, I used a lifelong interest in consciousness, leadership, and equity to create what I'd come to call SuperLoop Praxis—the process of using self-awareness, an understanding of biology, and personal responsibility to transform ourselves, our teams, and the larger organizations we are part of.

As I grew in experience, I began cementing the process of SuperLoop Praxis. These practices make use of how we relate to our beliefs, our biology, and our behavior to find and honor our humanity in our work. The Operationalizing of SuperLoop Praxis (the scaling, implementation, application, and reflection of that work) has an impact on the entire organization and allows for better productivity, more satisfaction among employees, and long-term stability and retention.

The large shift in perspective I underwent early in my career has deeply informed this work and allowed for massive, effective transformations within Little Sprouts. As an organization, we acknowledged that there wasn't an actual divide between our work lives and the rest of our lives—that our stress, gratification, and feelings didn't stop at some invisible barrier.

Transforming Little Sprouts taught us that we are, each of us, one human being with many facets. Pretending to "leave our problems at the door" intrinsically dishonors our fundamental humanity by pretending we can stop being human at work. Nobody with a sick child has ever been able to "leave it at the door," and I do not believe that a single human being on this earth has ever really been able to do so. We realized that we needed a more human model of work and organizational culture—and that this more human model could make us more effective.

We created this humancentric environment by providing our teams with consistent training, mentorship, on-the-job coaching, and Connection Time, where employees could utilize the expertise and education their peers could provide in a socialized learning environment. We created educational programs that centered on growing Actionable Awareness of executive function, financial literacy, conflict resolution, and even parenting skills. These programs gave us the ability to improve both at home and at work. And this made us better able to work. All our schools strove to provide access to the support services required to set team members up for the highest probability of success.

And it worked.

Our turnover was incredibly low, our satisfaction incredibly high, and the results began to win us awards across the United States.

Little Sprouts is a business that I would helm for more than thirty years and that I would continue to grow (even during the deepest years of the Wall Street crash between 2008 and 2012, when I grew Little Sprouts by a staggering 225 percent). The schools provided education for families across Massachusetts and New Hampshire, earning the US Department of Education Early Reading First Pre-schools Centers of Excellence Award. Little Sprouts was the only for-profit early education school to earn this national award for ten consecutive years. The Little Sprouts system of schools earned more than $10 million in innovation funding and partnered with the likes of the National Science Foundation, the Center for Public Broadcasting (CPB), WGBH, and the US Department of Education.

The model I used to reinvent and grow these schools was applicable far beyond education. As the schools I'd founded began to gain the interest of large investors, I began to systematically apply my models to other companies as a consultant—eventually founding G3 Works, the Golden Goose Group, which today is responsible for a transformation of scores of conscious high-growth global companies. As I built up to this, I shadowed leadership teams, acted as an advisor, and took exploratory meetings from across every industry I could find. By the time I'd made my multimillion-dollar exit from my first business, I had a roster of companies that had contracted me to help them transform their businesses with employee education, leadership training, and operational development.

The two terms that gradually emerged from my practices and consulting became SuperLoop Praxis and Operationalizing Consciousness, two practices based on mastering the positive feedback loops that link our bodies and our consciousness. I developed SuperLoop Praxis based on the philosophies I gleaned through years of thought leadership and from my experiences as the founder of Little Sprouts, Peace Love and Happiness Real Estate, Imajine That, and the Leadership and Literacy Foundation. Operationalizing Consciousness uses a system that integrates the tenets of Actionable Self-Awareness to create value in the form of increased Peer-to-Peer Accountability, deeper satisfaction, leadership from every role, and the practice of Healthy Conflict. SuperLoop Praxis is all about Operationalizing Consciousness and putting it to work as a practice in the world so that businesses can implement these skills and philosophies in a practical, scalable fashion. All of this results in greater access to our human potential so that we can maximize our performance across every level of our organizations. This is also an inclusive process, ensuring that those it represents are part of the process. We fully embrace the mantra of those seeking meaningful change that includes those who will be affected by that change—"nothing about us without us."

Empowered by these systems, we had everything needed to transform an organization and tap into its potential.

These are the skills and methods that made those schools and communities award-winning organizations. For more than forty years, the Little Sprouts schools earned accolades. These methods worked, and, importantly, it soon became clear that these methods worked for any organization that was able to enact them. Soon, there was a large demand not just for an expansion of the schools but for training in SuperLoop Praxis and in the innovative capital method I used to fund this education.

Navigating Our SuperLoop Framework

This book describes the process behind the major steps in engaging with SuperLoop Praxis. It begins with an exploration of central aspects of Operationalizing Consciousness and the SuperLoop concept; then, it describes the major educational steps an organization will undertake as part of the implementation process. Finally, for those who would like some expansion or to read about an idea with alternate phrasing, this book ends with a glossary including expanded explanations of the terminology that's been used throughout the process. Each chapter

SUPERLOOP

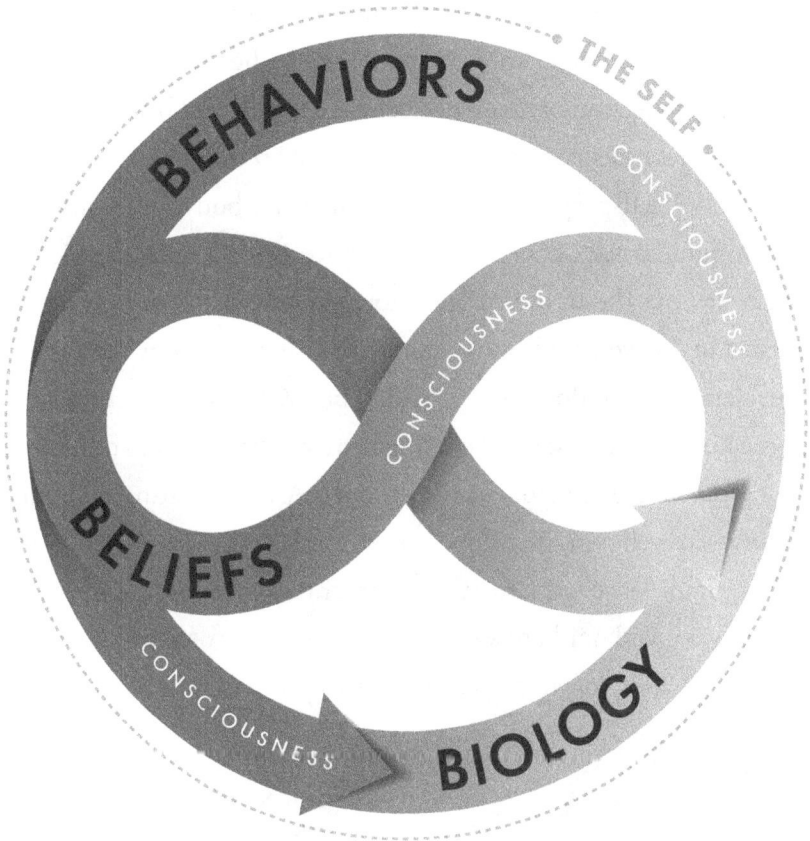

will include "Human Vibes," which are principles and mantras that help SuperLoop practitioners enact the ideas in this text as they work.

There are five core domains of Operationalized Consciousness that I will address as part of this book, and these are central to understanding the SuperLoop Praxis model and for the purpose of Operationalizing Consciousness within our organizations. All of these domains start out with personal skills, learning strategies, and leadership skills. They scale upward to an organization-wide operating system for transformation and growth.

The SuperLoop and SuperLoop Praxis

The core domains of Operationalizing Consciousness are the SuperLoop and SuperLoop-based Praxis. The SuperLoop is the constant connection between our beliefs, biology, and behavior—and the way these facets of existence combine to affect our consciousness. It is a self-perpetuating cycle where the body and consciousness influence each other. This influence impacts beliefs, biology, and behavior. These forces continuously create patterns for how we interact in the world. Although these might initially seem like a minor consideration, this domain is anything but. A computer is influenced by the kind of processor and cooling system it has—just as our minds are by our bodies (including our brains). An overheating computer doesn't run well—neither does a person who is boiling in stress and anxiety. In order to work to our best potential, we need to understand our software and our hardware and to become our own programmers rather than allowing all these elements to program us.

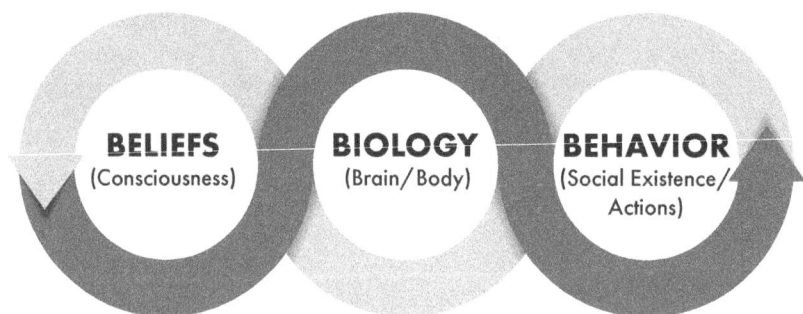

BELIEFS (Consciousness) — **BIOLOGY** (Brain/Body) — **BEHAVIOR** (Social Existence/Actions)

SuperLoop Praxis allows us to understand how our perceptions, our bodies, and our brains create our behavior. All of these factors affect our body (our heart pounds when we believe we are in danger—and then our adrenaline makes our perceptions fear based), creating a "loop" that can be *interrupted or processed* depending upon our understanding of the system. We spend much of our lives either ignoring or suppressing such information, but we can utilize a better understanding of our perceptions and bodies to engage in better conflict resolution, crisis management, and problem-solving.

SuperLoop is at the center of this practice because Operationalizing this biology, psychology, and sociology–based approach to inquiry increases our Actionable Awareness, allowing us to maximize our human potential and performance.

Dr. Carl Jung wrote, "The psychological rule says that when an inner situation is not made conscious, it happens outside, as fate."[8] In other words, until we make the unconscious into something conscious and addressable, it will direct our lives, and we will think it is the preordained nature of things.

Until you make the unconscious conscious, it will guide your life, and you will say it's just who you are. "I'm shy, I have a bad temper, I'm just a messy person, I say it how it is"—we begin to tell ourselves that we have an essential nature that cannot be changed.

But it can so long as we are paying attention to ourselves.

PERCEPTION

A critical domain of thought in the SuperLoop Praxis is a consideration of perception and how it informs our behaviors. Immediately, this may seem like a soft value, but perception is informed by our belief systems—both conscious and unconscious. Perception is the determining factor in how we gather information, how we translate it based on our own experience, and then how we choose to interpret that information.

---

8   Carl G. Jung, *Aion: Researches into the Phenomenology of the Self* (New Jersey: Princeton University Press, 1979).

Our perception is critical to how we perform. If we perceive ourselves as subservient and powerless when we have power, we miss out on opportunities. If we walk arrogantly into a tough situation, we might bungle what could have been managed. To be effective as professionals, we need as rigorous of a perception check model for our company culture (and really for our individual lives) as we do for gathering sales numbers or other performance telemetry.

We would not accept blind spots in any other area of our business. Still, when it comes to perception, we tend to operate on a level where perceived reality is occluded by our own biases and assumptions and the knee-jerk assumptions of our culture.

In order to engage in the kind of radical transformation SuperLoop Praxis offers, we will operate on the starting premise that perception is reality. This sounds like something from *The Matrix,* but this principle is repeated throughout history and most of philosophy, from Ancient Greece to Buddhism. Our beliefs about ourselves, about others, and about our actions dictate what we anticipate is possible and how we react to the world. We can't act on information we don't have, and we will act incorrectly when we believe information that is untrue—whether that untruth comes from internal or external sources.

RESPONDABILITY

Much of how individuals engage with the world is reactive. Learning to "respond," to act from a place of presence, rather than react, which is a borderline-involuntary behavior activated by behaviors we've learned from past circumstances, is critical to engaging. Differentiating between reactions and responses is a critical skill in bringing consciousness to an organization. This is an institutional skill as much as it is an individual skill.

Understanding our SuperLoop Praxis and how to process our perceptions teaches us to improve how we respond to stress, how we conduct ourselves in the face of leadership challenges, and how we handle conflict. Teaching ourselves how to practice RespondAbility also enables us to come up with new, innovative approaches to opportunities and challenges we encounter without being limited by our conditioned, cultural, or socialized reactions created by past experiences, thinking, and environments.

This domain of knowledge makes crisis management, conflict resolution, equity in structure, executive discernment, and strategic decisions a matter of conscious choice—by design—rather than something that is preordained by history, our biology, our culture, or some other circumstance that is trying to make a decision on our behalf by default and thereby forcing us to react.

HUMANCENTRIC ORGANIZATIONS

The fourth domain of SuperLoop Praxis is engaging with strategy as a whole human organization rather than what G3 broadly calls a "Human Resources" model. The original conception of Human Resources as an entity was to provide resources for a company's employees—to navigate the human elements of an organizational structure. This has gradually become untrue as profit maximization has overtaken business at the expense of equity and stability. The HR department has become an entity that is about administrative tasks and liability management rather than providing resources for humans.

A Humancentric Organization (HCO) is very different from a Human Resources organization, emphasizing that who we are at work is not truly separate from other roles in our lives and that the same human is engaging with both their work life and their personal life. An individual who is suffering cannot work effectively; they are impacted by that suffering, and that condition influences not only them but their entire organization.

On the subsistence level of the workforce, a team member who chronically worries about their basic existence, food insecurity, paying bills, and transportation will almost certainly not concentrate effectively on their work. They may exhibit responses we only see when humans enter survival mode: fight, flight, freeze, disassociate, or appease. To an outsider who is not aware of the context, they may appear detached, unapproachable, and agitated and appease the leadership by telling them only what they think leaders want to hear.

On the leadership level, someone who has allowed themselves to be driven into workaholism, isolation, or extreme anxiety by their high-level role will eventually buckle, physically or mentally, bringing their large influence with them and impacting others. The way we address leadership is extremely influenced by the structural power dynamics we see in the workplace. Executives and others in positions of power are typically given more grace when they are exhibiting survival behaviors as a response to their intense roles. "They have a lot on their plate" often justifies dysfunctional behavior or missing commitments. Conversely, an entry-level employee or middle manager does not get the same "hall pass" as they cope with the pressures they are dealing with in their lives. For many, personal lives are not considered appropriate for the workplace, and they are often told to "leave it at the door."

This Humancentric domain realizes that, like healthcare and retirement, there are systems we get to have in place for the benefit of the humans around us—an equitable endeavor that not only allows but expects us to be real with what's happening in our lives to the benefit of us, our teams, and our organizations.

CULTURE AND LEADERSHIP

SuperLoop Praxis deals with the idea of leadership differently than most leadership training; it deconstructs archaic, top-down notions of leading and engages, instead, with the concept of distributed leadership. When we engage with a system that has only a handful of leaders, it limits the agency and accountability of everyone who does not consider themselves to be a leader. Therefore, Peer-to-Peer Accountability and feedback are incredibly important to this methodology. The SuperLoop methodology teaches individuals to practice accountability and engagement by increasing agency and transparency. SuperLoop Praxis encourages organizations to make their employees aware of the financial, strategic, and organizational stakes related to their roles. People will support what they help to create.

An organization that has Operationalized Consciousness will be filled with employees who aren't just ticking off a box or filling in a spreadsheet because they've been told it's an obligation—they are engaging with an action whose purpose, context, and impact they understand. In the SuperLoop system, distributed leadership is intentionally developed by creating socialized learning, the process of learning from existing with our peers, and by Peer-to-Peer Accountability, which enables more productivity and agency than any single leader can muster. This methodology prevents a flourish-or-fail cult of personality that is often based on particular leaders and their perceived identities.

Finally, this book will end with a glossary of the terminology used in SuperLoop Praxis so that you can have a reference as you integrate these concepts into your work.

●   ●   ●

The impact G3 and SuperLoop Praxis have on individuals is dramatic. Some of the greatest joys of my life have been the chances to see the lives of those I've partnered with transformed by this process. To this day, I get notes and calls and get stopped in random places by participants who want to share how SuperLoop shifted their careers, marriages, parenting, and/or their entire thinking and responsibility for their personal power. This is as true for organizations as it is for individuals. Organizations with long-standing, seemingly intractable culture-deep issues find themselves transformed by their sudden ability to deal openly with hidden systemic problems or to break long-standing cultural norms that have been restrictive. They create innovation and productivity in places that seemed untenable in their old culture.

This is a practice and an art whose time has come. An incredible transformation is available to anyone who wants to address the major problems we face across our organizations. Just as important as the potential business rewards, these domains of knowledge address the real need we have as humans to be good people who do good work.

The finish line of the work in SuperLoop Praxis is clearly something our people and our organizations yearn for—we want to be productive, to celebrate the work we do, and to be challenged to new elevations that not only make us better teammates and employees but also a better life partner, parent, community member, neighbor, aunt, or uncle—all the important roles that we choose to be. We want to recognize our own humanity without struggling to push it aside for our jobs. Instead, our work should be a place that helps our humanity thrive—while also creating the great results we require to help the world thrive with our success.

This is a revolutionary project; it's something we'll use to transform the world. Now you, too, are part of forging a better way of working and living.

This isn't just something we *need* to do for ourselves and each other.

It's something we *get* to do. We are in service to a thriving humanity, starting with ourselves.

"School teaches us to conform, but the imagination teaches us to create. Authority teaches us to obey, but curiosity teaches us to question."

—GAVIN NASCIMENTO

CHAPTER ONE

PERCEPTION IS REALITY

The Body Shop was a company that engaged with progressive business since its inception in 1976. Although it was recently purchased and dismantled, it was a powerful forty-eight-year business with an incredible legacy. It was one of the first corporations founded on social responsibility. The founder, Dame Anita Roddick, believed in the revolutionary principle that business could be a source for good. Roddick traveled the globe to find ethically sourced ingredients and to understand the conditions under which ingredients were created, undertaking journeys into Sub-Saharan deserts to examine shea farming or to find an alternative for the whale oil that was commonly used in the beauty industry at the time.

The Body Shop was the first corporation to partner with Greenpeace to stop Amazon Forest destruction and to embrace the Save the Whales campaign. They created the term and model of Community Fair Trade, still considered a part of the brand's DNA. The Body Shop was a beacon for changing perceptions toward beauty standards, what is considered "masculine" or "feminine," and ultimately in empowering women (and really all humans) with its business practices and products.

I still vividly remember meeting with The Body Shop for the first time in 2019. Their New York headquarters was gorgeous and minimalist. There wasn't any clutter. There were pictures of Dame Roddick across the walls, with quotes that embodied the values of The Body Shop's culture superimposed over images of her exploits. I still remember one of these: "To succeed, you have to believe in something with such a passion that it becomes reality"—a very fitting precursor to the work G3 would do alongside The Body Shop.

There were even calls to action on the bathroom walls and in the stalls. The scent of Satsuma orange blossoms hung in the air, the smell of one of their most beloved body lotion preparations. Much of the media around the conference room was celebrating that they had begun the transition to being 100 percent plastic free. I was struck by how long it had been since Anita had started her mission of equity (a legacy that lives on, since its founding in 1976). All of it was so inspiring that I welled up with tears before we'd even begun. *My people,* I thought.

The body language and nonverbal communication of the leadership team reminded me of my early days in the teaching profession— they were the faces of eager kindergartners who were beaming with curiosity and ready to learn. They were in love with their mission, with the world, and they wanted to do even more than they were already doing. I practically felt everything falling into place even before we'd begun. I knew that the level of commitment I was experiencing meant that we would achieve what The Body Shop was setting out to do.

"PERCEPTION IS REALITY": One of the Human Vibes, which is also the title of this chapter, is that perception is one of the main determining factors in how we are affected by the world (and how we affect it). Our beliefs about ourselves, others, and the world determine what we believe is possible and how we engage with stimuli.

The Body Shop had contracted G3 to help Operationalize its drive toward being a conscious business and to lead in advancing their mission to increase the impact of their values of inclusion and belonging. They wanted to increase their retention, revolutionize their hiring policies by beginning an Inclusive Hiring system, and reengage with Dame Roddick's vision by partnering with system-impacted individuals in the global communities they served to provide upskilling and uplifting. The company had been purchased by L'Oréal in 2006 for $652 million, and then been sold to Natura in 2017 for $1.1 billion.

This process put them through a bit of an identity crisis. The larger brand of L'Oréal didn't have the same values as The Body Shop. They didn't source ingredients in the way Roddick did, and they might have engaged in animal testing,[9] something that Roddick abhorred and actively fought against. Roddick spent the last years of her life navigating this acquisition, trying to make sure that The Body Shop retained its values despite the ownership by such a different brand.

However, the recent purchase by Natura had given The Body Shop a new lease on life. They had a chance to recreate themselves and

---

9   Robert Booth, "Activists Call Body Shop Boycott," *Guardian*, March 17, 2006, https://
www.theguardian.com/business/2006/mar/17/retail.animalrights, accessed March
30, 2008.

to re-sanctify their values. They wanted to address their inclusion and belonging principles as well as getting back to their roots of engaging with suppliers globally. They wanted to ensure this process was Operationalized throughout their global efforts—starting with Inclusive Hiring. They found, however, that something was stopping them from fully applying their values to certain aspects of their business—especially when it came to recruiting and hiring. They wanted to continue to do good work and to provide good products while also being good people. This desire led them to contact G3 to develop a comprehensive strategy to transform their culture, practices, and operating systems that both reflected their commitment to the communities and customers and to creating a life-affirming workplace for the entire team.

G3 was commissioned on behalf of The Body Shop to design the Inclusive Hiring strategy, create an implementation plan, and execute a comprehensive advancement in organizational development and operations using SuperLoop Praxis. This enabled a bold transformation in The Body Shop by analyzing and recreating the systems that were affecting retention, recruiting, and important KPIs related to the completion of their deliverables in roles across the entire organization. I explained G3's SuperLoop Praxis system and its comprehensive inside-out approach. All of these operations needed to be aligned with their five-year strategic plan and their current learning and development models, which made the exercise even more challenging.

Through this process with G3, The Body Shop hired more than 1,400 system-impacted individuals, a substantial (more than 25 percent) addition to a company with a staff of just over 5,000 employees. On top of that, this major hiring took place during the peak of the COVID-19 pandemic and during a time when companies were having extreme difficulties hiring employees at all—let alone retaining them. The results were definitive and dramatic, and they didn't come from new technology or from a reorganization by some efficiency expert. It was cocreated by a small group of committed humans at G3 and The Body Shop who embodied their vision to impact a fairer humanity.

One of the major keys to working with The Body Shop was ultimately teaching them to redesign their organizational perspective of several critical areas of their company—especially when it came to hiring, retention, education, and how and when they defined a practice as successful in the context of their culture.

One of the most critical steps to engaging with a shift in perception is to examine where that perception even comes from—where's the data that is creating our worldview, and how is it being gathered? The Body Shop needed consistent data on how its employees perceived the company individually, collectively, and organizationally. Eventually, we identified that they needed to shift how they approached hiring, recruitment, and comprehensive employee development to truly engage with their values and experience increased outcomes.

Like all journeys into perception, this involved interrogating the assumptions they made about the world. As they examined their perspective, they revolutionized their strategies, organizational alignment, and goals, in pursuit of answering one question—Can we be good humans and operate a good business?

Change the Way You See the World, and the World You See Changes

Knowing how our perceptions influence us is the start of Operationalizing Consciousness inside our organizations by applying SuperLoop

Praxis. We then put that consciousness to work so that it benefits every community member involved in the culture—both inside and out.

Change the way you see the world, and the world you see changes. *Perception is reality.* This is true for individuals, teams, and entire organizations or cultures.

Perception is something many business leaders might see as a "soft" skill. It's something that isn't easily modeled out, and it's also something that our traditional style of command-and-control leadership has taught us is not really something we need to consider outside of being an influential individual or someone who is a charismatic leader. At the most, many companies think of perception in terms of branding, advertising, and optics. They think of perception as being an external tool to monetize when it is most definitely a powerful internal tool for the individual, the organization, and a culture.

The fields of public relations, advertising, behavioral economics, and media are all based around creating culture by influencing perceptions. They're the business vertices in which we see people work with perception the most. Because of these industries, we see this as a one-way connection: a person gets influenced, then they buy a product, believe a point of view, or consume something in the intended way. This has been the case since Edward Bernays, who established the field of modern public relations using the theories of his uncle, Sigmund Freud, to shift public perception in support of the tobacco industry and to inculcate the agricultural companies that were operating merciless "Banana Republics," corporate-run dictatorships, abroad.[10]

We know that these are powerful, profitable industries and forces because they're able to influence perception. To lend some context, these industries are worth more than $106.93 billion as of

---

10   Peter Chapman, *BANANAS: How the United Fruit Company Shaped the World* (New York: Canongate, 2007).

2023.[11] What we don't often think about is the implication this has in regard to our perceptions; they are extremely powerful, and they are malleable—but they are also something we can influence on our own. We are responsible for our own perceptions, and we can collectively craft something powerful if we work on our perceptions and the resulting beliefs as a group.

HUMAN VIBE: "PERCEPTION RUNS TWO WAYS."

Many people unconsciously hold the idea that our perception of the world will be shared by others, but we must practice the fact that the perception of others will vary from our own. The idea that media influences the perceptions of a passive audience (and thereby dictates that audience's reality) is called "the injection model."[12] This is a model of media consumption that has held on since the early days of public relations and advertising, but one that is now considered too simplistic. Media is now seen as being a persuasive effort given to an audience that actively negotiates the information with which they are presented. Audiences accept, reject, or negotiate their reading of media sources, and this influences their own perception of the world. Inside of organizations and culture, much of our perception of reality comes from media and from written and spoken communication—whether that's employee handbooks and policies, internal messages, external advertising, or training.

11   "Public Relations Global Market Report," Business Research Company, accessed June 6, 2024, https://www.thebusinessresearchcompany.com/report/public-relations-global-market-report.

12   Brian L. Ott and Robert L. Mack, *Critical Media Studies: An Introduction*, 3rd ed. (Hoboken: Wiley-Blackwell, 2020).

If organizations are not actively considering the impact of perception, its leadership might believe that they can dictate culture with the rhetoric of their mission and value statements and that this culture will immediately fall into place. Operationalizing Consciousness inside of an organization requires that we understand how individuals, groups, and the wider culture are in a dynamic state of development and decision-making and not just a pliable, passive group. An organization invested in developing Actionable Awareness in its members will consistently work toward an effective culture with increased performance outcomes, both quantitative and qualitative.

If we are not aware of our perceptions, if we do not *own* them by taking 100 percent responsibility for them, we allow forces outside of ourselves to influence us on an unconscious and subconscious level, by default. Our perceptions are the foundations of our beliefs, yet we rarely work to own and influence our perceptions for ourselves. We hold a belief that we are determined by these perceptions rather than owning that they influence us and that we can influence them. If we aren't aware of our own perceptions, we are at the mercy of those who are. If we aren't aware of our own realities, we can't effectively influence the realities of the groups around us or be mindful of our influence on the wider culture.

Our perceptions are the foundations of our beliefs.

In most aspects of our lives, the way a person perceives reality is, in fact, their reality. Their individual perceptions affect those around them (and their perceptions, in turn, are affected by those around them). This spreads out from groups to the whole. On an interpersonal level, this even comes down to the fact that our hormones and neurobiology are influenced by the biology of those around us through our mirror neurons. Our reality comes down to the information we receive, the way our bodies handle sensory input, and the circumstances we are surrounded by. It then becomes a matter of the social and cultural interactions that cement this set of perceptions as reality when we translate all of it into our experience of our own existence. On top of all these psychosocial realities, there is a biological component to perception and its social effect upon the individual known as mirror neurons, suggesting that we are affected biologically by what we perceive (an idea that will receive more depth and attention later in our discussion).

You're already well aware of how important perception is to our day-to-day lives and identity, even if it's not something you actively think about often. Let's make a hypothetical examination of this idea—consider an individual who only reads negative news stories and generally only talks to like-minded people. On the individual level, this consumption might lead to thoughts that will likely make their reality feel sad, threatening, or desperate. They are immune to good news because of the immense evidence of how bad things are. Disastrously, they ignore solutions that fall outside of their limited, skeptical worldview. They live in a grim world, and a grim world isn't likely to provide solutions. We know these people; they've even got a cultural name coined by the internet: doomers.

A person who focuses exclusively on environmental destruction, for instance, won't hear about positive developments in climate science. They might shoot down new ideas in the face of their self-imposed, doomed personal reality. This person would likely project this into their world, influencing the perceptions of those around them. They would likely also carry this hopelessness into work, affecting their ability to tackle tasks and even perhaps their entire organization by way of influencing their teams and those attempting to work with or for them. They might then influence their culture with this pessimism.

This is an identity, like many, that begins with our thoughts or, more specifically, the frequency and prominence of our thoughts.

A person who consumes only positive news might, on the other hand, find that their perception of reality is too rose-colored to serve them well. They might not prepare for difficulties and have a resistance to engaging in conflict even when they should. They might not know new strategies are needed because they don't perceive the signs that a current strategy is failing. On the "WE" level, they might not feel the need to contribute to solutions or discuss problems (or perceive them at all!), and this might lead to stagnation on the cultural level as well as a personal disconnect from possible solutions.

We all know people like this, but very few people actually want to be like this. Being deliberate with our thoughts, therefore, becomes a much better option than allowing for the default fear and reactivity.

Each of these hypothetical scenarios involves perceptions that have dictated a certain kind of reality in an extreme way, and each of them has led to similar negative consequences by a different route. The perception of the individual in each hypothetical has limited their reality.

This possibility demonstrates how perception is of paramount importance, and it radiates outward to systems outside of the individual. Carol Dweck, a leading thinker in this area, has labeled the consequences and benefits of these two approaches to the world as either a "fixed mindset" or a "growth mindset."[13] Ellen Galinsky further expanded on these notions by outlining the process by which we can make a possibilities mindset actionable by using her concept of a "possibility mindset." A possibility mindset sees change as a challenge to be embraced rather than a threat, where change is less possible.

---

13   Carol Dweck, *Mindset: The New Psychology of Success* (New York: Ballantine Books, 2016).

These worldviews described above represent two different paths to what is called a fixed mindset. A fixed mindset is a state of mind that seeks stasis. As the examples above illustrate, this condition keeps an individual from changing according to the conditions of the world around them. This can be a state for individuals, teams, or even entire organizations or cultures. It is a refusal to develop, and it can ultimately become the death knell of an organization if it takes hold and is not countered. All innovation involves change, and the fixed mindset is incapable of growth because it is avoidant of recognizing its own limitations and blind spots.

The opposite of this is what is called a possibilities mindset. A possibilities mindset is an active, dynamic state of mind that embraces change and seeks to grow and transform. SuperLoop Praxis encourages a growth state and possibilities mindset by dispelling the flawed perceptions that create blind spots, enhancing the way in which the I/WE/ALL collaborates, and fostering pathways for clear communication. Individuals (and teams/organizations) with a possibilities mindset are able to evolve because they embrace risk and welcome Healthy Conflict, which those with a fixed mindset are unable to do.

Evolving Mindsets: Feedback, Evolved

"If you tell me the truth about myself, you just might be saving my life."[14]

---

14   Marcus Buckingham and Ashley Goodall, "The Feedback Fallacy," *Harvard Business Review*, April–May Issue, 2019, https://hbr.org/2019/03/the-feedback-fallacy.

What keeps us in a fixed mindset, and how can we engage in a possibilities mindset? Why is a fixed mindset a problem for so many individuals, teams, and organizations? How can we move from a fixed mindset to what Ellen Galinsky has defined as a "possibility mindset"—a frame of perception that allows us to adapt and change with direct action after we have engaged with a possibilities mindset?[15]

One of the main phenomena that keeps us stuck in a particular perception is known as a blind spot. Used in this context, this is not referring to a loss of sight or a vision impairment. Rather, it refers to the fact that all of us have a spot on our retina that is incapable of transmitting visual information. We cannot perceive this spot, and yet, if an object falls within this visual range, we will not be aware of this object.

This analogy and terminology fit our purposes because organizations are allowed to reach states where they are incapable of perceiving the issues that are impairing their operation. Largely, organizations become subject to blind spots when they are unable to utilize perceptions outside of their own. In the case of The Body Shop, their competitors were unable to discern that they had a blind spot when it came to hiring, learning, and development and were thus unable to create an innovative solution for finding job applicants in a hiring market with new demands.

On the team and individual levels, we need the perception of others if we do not want to be stuck in our own biases. The SuperLoop Praxis utilizes a process known as "FeedForward," which is a practice that invites the perspective of another and enables us to work outside of our previous blind spots and perceptual limitations. This, in turn,

---

15   Ellen Galinsky, *The Breakthrough Years: A New Scientific Framework for Raising Thriving Teens* (New York: Flatiron Books, 2024), Kindle edition.

enables an organizational culture to access their maximum potential and productivity better than their previous limited worldview allowed.

Most businesses and teams attempt to encourage growth and change by using feedback, but feedback is actually an inherently unreliable and generally negative way to negotiate teamwork and change perceptions. The way an individual experiences feedback is influenced very heavily by their past experiences and by their interpretation of present facts. If you haven't had the lived experience of an individual, you cannot give them applicable feedback. Rather than engaging in traditional feedback, we must seek to engage in an exchange of perspectives instead of one-sided feedback.

As Marcus Buckingham and Ashley Goodall wrote in the *Harvard Business Review,* "The only source of information on which humans are an unimpeachable authority is themselves."[16] Human beings are inherently operating at an experiential deficit when they deal with another person. This is a barrier that cannot be crossed; we simply cannot be another person. So when we provide feedback, which is ultimately an assertion of our perspective, we are superimposing our perspective over the other, more authentic and accurate experience of another person.

This isn't to be confused with offering instruction, which means providing of facts that are inherently valuable. Imparting knowledge is critical to success. Feedback, however, is often dealing with the qualitative level of reality—even when it seems like it is not. Our perceptions often feel unimpeachable to ourselves.

Feedback ignores the truth that our perceptions can be flawed. If we accept that feedback is subjective, that we are usually applying

---

16   Marcus Buckingham and Ashley Goodall, "The Feedback Fallacy," *Physician Leadership Journal,* March 2019, https://www.physicianleaders.org/articles/the-feedback-fallacy.

motive, reaching a conclusion, or extrapolating based on our assumptions, then the act of giving feedback is inherently an assertion of the perspective of the person giving the feedback.

Take, for example, a supervisor who gives their direct report feedback about missing deadlines and states that the individual needs to be more organized and rigorous in their scheduling. This feedback assumes that the speaker knows the reason for the work not being completed, that they understand the cause, and that said cause doesn't need further input from the person being evaluated to create the agreed-upon business results.

The person who received this feedback might have additional information that needs to be interpreted. They are missing some critical element from another team, they suffered a death in their family, or they were not actually responsible for the element on which they are being given feedback. Ultimately, the mitigating factor doesn't matter for our discussion here so much as it matters that the supervisor doesn't know the actual reason for the missed deliverable. They now can't rectify the systemic problem that is slowing down their productivity—all because their perceptions led them to the belief that there is certainty about why this deadline was missed.

THE PAST IS ALWAYS PRESENT

In addition to the fact that feedback can lead to incomplete information, it can also lead to different reactions depending on patterns we've encountered in our past experiences—an individual who receives feedback on something might react negatively if they experienced a childhood with a harsh parent or if they've experienced toxic workplaces in the past. The same piece of feedback given to a different person might have a totally different connotation for the receiver if they've previously received positive mentorship.

Since our past informs us, we are very likely to perceive the very same set of circumstances differently if we grew up with supporting parents who offered criticism and reinforcement in equal measure. They focused on the strengths of their children rather than their weaknesses. Something that sounds harsh to one set of ears could just as well be heard as a supportive prompt by another. Directive statements become something they can align with, a helpful suggestion given the benefit of the doubt.

The human brain tracks for certainty; it will seek out patterns that we are used to. This will lock us into biological and behavioral patterns that repeat our past experiences—which will also dictate our reactions by locking us into the reactions we already know. The only way to avoid reinforcing the same patterns throughout our lives is to be conscious of these forces and how they influence the choices we make. Why do people marry spouses similar to their parents? Why do some people seem to seek out conflict while others avoid it? They are recreating the patterns of certainty that have thus far been their reality. These are the situations their neurobiology finds comfortable.

Mindfulness of our own perceptions is powerful. An individual who is aware of how subjective their reality is has the power to completely shift reality. A person who is aware of the influence that their past experiences are having upon their mindset might be able to stop and ask themselves whether they are properly interpreting the information they are receiving (G3 calls this "interrogating our reality"). Is this really negativity? Or am I prone to interpreting words and behavior as being negative due to my past experiences? What information outside of myself can I use to influence my perception of these circumstances? Why am I being triggered by this situation?

HUMAN VIBE: "EMOTIONS ARE A PERSONAL RESPONSIBILITY." We must be responsible for our own feelings and understand our own emotional wiring. As an individual, you have the ability to understand and meet your own needs while also understanding and meeting the needs of another. Emotions are energy in motion—literal electricity and chemicals, and this energy cannot be ignored.

FeedForward

A technique known as FeedForward breaks the already-existing cycle of an individual, team, or organization's inculcated perceptions and frees them from these cycles of reacting to feedback and lingering in inescapable blind spots.

"FeedForward": FeedForward is the process of sharing perspectives, one to one and collectively, and communicating via a series of strategic prompts rather than presenting another person with a piece of information that pushes them backward (as is implied by feed*back)*. This term uses language that is aware of how it might be perceived, and it is an example of how an awareness of perception can be built into the language and practices of a culture.

FeedForward uses these prompts:

- FeedForward Prompt: "What I love about working with you …"
    - This is critical because it allows an individual to authentically acknowledge the skill and impact of their colleague as the opening part of the interaction. This also connects the speaker to how the person in the dialogue has con-

tributed to their professional life and the organizational results.

- FeedForward Prompt: "What I think you can do to increase your impact ..."

    □ This allows for a constructive path forward toward improvement. It also acknowledges the individual's role on the "I" level, in their team and as a member of the organization. It is the beginning stages of internalizing peer-to-peer accountability.

- FeedForward Prompt: "A pattern that I observe that you may or may not be aware of is ... and the impact that has is ..."

    □ Since self-perception is so difficult, it takes a collective effort. This is a chance for individuals to become aware of patterns that affect their results. This is a chance to engage in peer-to-peer learning and reinforcement of knowledge. This is where blind spots that are impacting relationships and results are brought to the light.

- FeedForward Recipient Response Prompt: "What I hear you saying is that .... Am I getting everything?"

    □ The final step in the FeedForward process is for the person receiving information to rephrase what they've heard to make sure that there is a shared understanding of what's been discussed.

I originally created FeedForward to Operationalize the practice of peer-to-peer accountability that uses the perspectives of everyone involved in the act of communication. Operationalizing effective, clear communication in this way is the first method to transform a business. The executives I work with frequently cite poor communication and a lack of accountability as the two biggest problems their workforce faces. What I found is that problems with communication do not frequently arise from a lack of knowledge or awareness about what their teammates are doing—in fact, they usually can tell you straight out what trends are at work in their teams. The communication difficulties arise from the fact that people don't have the competency (or the permission) to communicate the information they have in an effective manner.

They don't, for instance, communicate that a peer is slowing their team down by being too fastidious, or that they themselves need to change the workflow to be more effective. Once an organization has developed a FeedForward practice, they create an environment where it's expected that we are consistently leveling each other up. It creates the practice of Peer-to-Peer Accountability where *we are all collectively responsible for the results of the team and the individual team members' continued growth.*

FeedForward should be consistently used to create the expectation that perception will be shared and discussed. This technique breaks down the existing hierarchy and unifies I/WE/ALL by encouraging communication and eliminating breakdowns in strategies. Where a traditional hierarchy (and feedback) relies on people not talking back, FeedForward relies on communication at all levels.

This process enables us to continually engage with other perceptions and to develop the courage to Say the Unsaid. This also creates the expectation that those engaging in FeedForward will be able to engage with the perception of others while not judging the process or perception being shared. The very core of this process is honoring the perception of others, which also means that we are honoring their beliefs and realities in a way that widens the field of communication and therefore widens the number of solutions, increases the possible outcomes, and addresses ideas that would normally be neglected.

The FeedForward process also allows for individuals to evolve. Our initial perception of an individual is often locked in. FeedForward constantly "pings" the other individual and gets updates on their current perception/reality. They are not locked into a first impression, roles, or previous statements as in the traditional hierarchical mode of interaction.

The FeedForward system is dynamic, where the traditional hierarchy and a traditional feedback-driven culture is one of stagnation, one where we are tracking for certainty and work under the very fragile illusion that we are in a static world. It's a paradoxical worldview where we expect institutional growth but constantly rely on individuals staying the same for the sake of our own comfort.

I, WE, and ALL

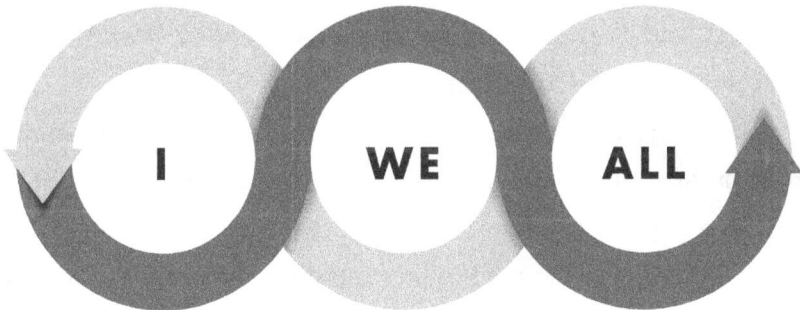

Being mindful of different scales of perception is necessary for any kind of effectiveness and for any transformation. In the vocabulary of SuperLoop systems (and adapted from the work of Dr. Ken Wilbur[17])

---

17   Ken Wilber, *No Boundary: Eastern and Western Approaches to Personal Growth* (Boulder: Shambhala Publications, 1979).

this is referred to as the I/WE/ALL model. Each of these levels is intertwined with the others, and each needs to be considered and attended to for the individual, their team, and their organization to flourish. Individuals tend to naturally focus on one or two of these levels more than they do the others, and a perception of all three grants a large amount of flexibility in how we implement strategy and engage with our organization.

The "I" level of perception deals with a focus on the individual level. It's influenced by the information we consume, the way our bodies react to our past experiences, the way we internalize the current facts around us (more on this in the next chapter), and the choices we make about how we interpret our surroundings. What do I perceive to be urgent? What is unimportant? What's positive? Negative? Who is my friend? My enemy?

These choices form the lens through which we look at the world. Is the sign my company has posted asking me to "use less paper" an indicator that my company cares about the environment and our Earth? Or is it a sign that they are cutting corners, withholding resources, and don't care whether they impede upon my workflow or what supplies I need as an employee?

My frame of reference, my past experiences, and the decisions I make on how I translate such information will determine my reality (and, to a large degree, how I feel about my team and my company).

For example, what used to be a fun diversion can be a tiresome task if we do it too often—or if we feel we're forced to do it. The salad we hated as a child is delicious in adulthood. Neither conclusion is incorrect, and nothing about the salad or the previously fun hobby has changed. The only thing that's changed is our perception of these things, which has subsequently become our reality.

PERCEPTION IS REALITY

The "WE" level of perception is the level of perception that includes a team, division, family or other group with a common goal or task. The WE level of perception will influence the way a team approaches a project or goal, their attitude toward undertaking problem-solving, the way in which information is received, and how they will uphold Peer-to-Peer Accountability. This level has a high susceptibility to be influenced by individuals, and the attitude of a team can easily radiate outward and affect an entire organization or culture. The culture of a team can, conversely, very much affect the individual—they are susceptible to peer pressure, team inertia, and the social dynamics of a team. Nobody wants to be the canary in the coal mine; they "go along to get along."

The person who is a people pleaser values the WE more than the I or the ALL (or potentially more than themselves, sacrificing the I level). These people might overwork for the sake of the team, which hurts them and the institution, and ultimately even their team when they work themselves to burnout, resentment, and inefficiency. Those with "the disease to please" notoriously do not hold others accountable by setting clear boundaries, which is not sustainable.

A team's attitude toward an action can reinforce (or undermine) individual perspectives. Returning to the example of the "use less paper" sign, the dynamic of a team becomes critical. A "WE-focused" set of leaders among that team will lead to a more positive interpretation. If this team tends to engage other perspectives and view themselves as a part of a collective, an individual in that team might be influenced to receive that paper-preservation note in the best spirit possible because they are being granted another perspective.

If, on the other hand, a team perceives themselves to be under fire from the management, at risk as a group, or that they are underserved by the organization (the ALL), such a message might not only be received negatively by an individual on the team, but the members of the team might complain to each other, might hoard supplies, or might disregard the notice willfully—leading to a detrimental effect on everyone (the ALL) and an unsafe environment for the individual (the I).

Several questions arise when we're mindful of team-level perception. How does this team perceive their responsibilities? What do they think of leadership? Or their own role when it comes to being leaders? What are their internal goals? What is the relationship of the individual to the team? What's the relationship of the team to the wider organization?

The "ALL" level of perception includes both the company and the wider culture to which the company belongs. All cultures have conceptions that influence their reality. Does an organization have values that it actively enacts in the world? Does it Operationalize these internally? What are the customs and mores of said culture? What are their conceptions of what is appropriate or inappropriate? Acceptable or unacceptable? Professional or unprofessional? Do these conclusions and conventions serve the missions of the team and of the individuals? Is everyone on all levels practicing what they preach? Do individuals and teams serve the mission of the ALL?

In order for human beings to contribute, they must have their needs met. The I/WE/ALL also scales backward; the needs of the institution must also be met for the individual to be effective.

Returning to the example of our fictitious company with its "use less paper" sign, the ALL level of perception becomes particularly important for how teams and individuals might translate this information. A company like The Body Shop, an organization that is committed to the practices of inclusion, teamwork, and a social and environmental justice mission to better the world through the paths by which they engage with their partners and their people, is much more likely to have a positive reception for such a message. They are demonstrating that their values go beyond slogans on the wall or a note about paper usage.

A company that doesn't consistently embody their values and instead focuses on only its moment-to-moment operation often ends up marginalizing the individuals they are trying to inspire. A company that does not "walk their talk" by embodying their values will receive a totally different reaction to such a message. The leadership of a company can contribute to how such a sign influences the I/WE/ALL.

A blunt, generally dispassionate company will be perceived on face value. The blunt "use less paper" sign will be interpreted as abrasive or disconnected. A sign from a company that holds strong values on the ALL will be perceived as radically distinct. An organization that engages with the environmental cost of their operations and enacts a commitment to being green, for instance, will be received in a completely different manner. While this seems like an obvious conclusion, the important factor is that the perception of the role of the ALL will have a heavy, inescapable influence on the I/WE levels of an organization.

The moment-to-moment elements of this interaction of the sign in our example aren't the emphasis here—what matters is that an organization must be cognizant of how they are Operationalizing their awareness of the I/WE/ALL in their actions.

The most important element in creating trust at the foundation of the interactions between these relational levels is consistency— a consistent, reliable commitment to the values and strategies the company espouses in its culture and communications. Keeping these commitments becomes the Unsaid statement that our organization is making in the eyes of both the I/WE level and outsiders.

If you say you're a green company, you need to be green. A lack of reliability will quickly lead to a negative perception, and that perception will lead to a breakdown in the relational levels of the I/WE/ALL. The lack of trust between executives and their team members is the price we pay for the chronic systemic inequities in corporations. This inequality has gone on long enough that it has become a constant sentiment of popular culture that "working for the man" has a price. As always, these breakdowns result in a lose-lose situation.

When there are breakdowns in the relational levels, the divisions between these levels manifests as isolating behavior. A team leader who is overly focused on the WE might think or say, "That sounds good for the overall company, but I need to protect my team," if they are in an organization that has a breakdown between the WE and the ALL, which optimally impacts the results for the company. An individual who has a breakdown between themselves and their team might decide they are looking out for themselves first, leading to a hesitancy to commit, practice Peer-to-Peer Accountability, and take risks. This fault could stem from any number of levels, but it manifests with the same outcome—an attempt at isolation for the I/WE levels followed by an inability to pursue the goals of the ALL.

To illustrate in practice how interconnected these levels are, consider the fact that an employee who is annoyed by this sign has a choice as to whether they communicate this to their team and their leadership, and even in *how* they communicate this unease. Do they make it a statement that reminds the team of their values, or does it become a confrontation? Do they propose an alternative sign, or do they merely slander the leadership? Do they simply remain silent and "go along to get along"? The levels are inextricably interconnected and immediately influence each other.

Individuals tend to gravitate toward one or two of these relational levels, but being locked into just one level creates a lack of consideration/awareness/value for the other levels and will create a systemic breakdown if left unchecked. What tends to happen is that midlevel managers are great on the I/WE, but they are not naturally strong at the ALL. They promote and fight for individuals and teams but lose the consideration of the overall strategy (my team worked hard but didn't hit goals—resulting in layoffs).

When they do think about the ALL, they tend to get promoted to executive roles. Executives tend to look at the ALL to the exclusion of the other levels, which might involve not examining workload, working conditions, or material realities for the individual or team. For true transformation, every role needs to be considered. The ALL needs to be set up for individuals and teams to prosper. Teams and individuals need to be aware and informed regarding the ALL if their actions are meant to contribute to it. Organization relations are a dynamic dance; they feed off each other, and every level needs to engage in FeedForward and other strategies that link them to each relational level. This is similar to a constant SWOT (strengths, weaknesses, opportunities, and threats) analysis, a consideration of every level that helps or hinders stability and productivity.

HARNESSING THE I/WE/ALL

To unify the I/WE/ALL of an institution, an organization must be set up to serve all three levels of the I/WE/ALL. If the individual or teams do not have the supplies, support, or communication to carry out the goals of the ALL, they simply cannot do so, and they will struggle and burn out as they try. The culture of the ALL needs to be set up for learning and change. This means consistently investing in the development of team members, improving communication, and Operationalizing the development they receive. Mentoring, coaching, and supporting processes are the critical systems that allow for an effective, deliberately developmental organization. A deliberately developmental organization integrates personal and professional growth into its daily operations, fostering a culture of continuous learning, transparency, and trust by embedding that development into everyday work.[18]

A company that wants to center their customer service experience needs to engage with special training that is reinforced with Praxis—*practice that exercises our values with real action.* In order to create maximum buy-in across the I/WE, the individuals and teams in an organization need to know that this training will matter and have an impact. The commitment from the ALL in the form of these resources, implementation, and reflection is a clear message that this education will matter.

This is an important differentiation because an organization must allocate the resources for this training and practice, budget the time for it, and provide employees with the space to enact that training as a practice. As this process occurs, an organization has to measure the results and use that measurement to continue adapting so that negative or counter-productive behaviors do not creep in. Engaging in training alone is just imparting knowledge with no way to use that knowledge, and it will ultimately wither if it goes unused. Training without practice is the equivalent of throwing money out the window. Eventually, with practice, we will find that the new elements we want to implement have become the air we breathe. At G3, we offer consultative services, including training, yet one of our Human Vibes is that

---

18   Robert Kegan and Lisa Laskow Lahey, *An Everyone Culture: Becoming a Deliberately Developmental Organization* (Boston: Harvard Business Review Press, 2016).

"training does not work." Organizations don't use this vibe because training doesn't actually work—rather, it's because we have a flawed perception of what training is and we want to dispel the reliance people have on the flawed model of training that's become traditional.

Many are frustrated with the notion of training because they've experienced training that is not followed up with action and resources. The training in SuperLoop Praxis is based on creating sustainable learning practices that are built into the day-to-day operations of a company. Our consulting builds in practices to immediately apply the work instead of just presenting ideas that can be ignored.

For one company, this space to Operationalize their values will be considering the qualitative as much as the quantitative. Hypothetically, this might mean not tracking call times at the expense of service—and listening to employees when they state that tracking call times is impacting their performance. For many companies, this means providing technology appropriate to the tasks they are expected to complete. This means making sure that individuals, teams, and the overall culture of the company are all aware of and aligned with this goal and provide key goals associated with their desired outcomes.

This doesn't mean abandoning the quantitative or qualitative elements of running a business. This means we need to use both! The quantitative is sometimes easy to measure, but the qualitative is just as critical. Measure call times, but make sure that client and employee satisfaction are measured too. Then adjust for both.

For The Body Shop, transforming its developmental organization into a deliberately developmental culture meant consistent training and educational opportunities, accessible mentorship, and role practice that occurred both asynchronously and synchronously. It meant providing the funds, time, and communication needed for this training. It meant addressing material concerns like providing electronics for training and hiring. It meant Operationalizing this training by communicating goals, changing their hiring process, and tracking the results of these actions. The company made sure that the entire organization was aware of the truth that its values were also its strategic priorities.

And the results of all this commitment, risk, and effort led to a transformation that was completely revolutionary. The Body Shop would use this Actionable Awareness to enact its values from the ground up.

"Fitting in is one of the greatest barriers to belonging. Fitting in is about assessing a situation and becoming who you need to be in order to be accepted. Belonging, on the other hand, doesn't require us to change who we are; it requires us to be who we are."

—BRENÉ BROWN, *DARING GREATLY*[19]

---

19   Brené Brown, *Daring Greatly: How the Courage to Be Vulnerable Transforms the Way We Live, Love, Parent, and Lead* (New York: Gotham Books, 2012).

"Business shapes the world. It is capable of changing society in almost any way you can imagine."

—DAME ANITA RODDICK

CHAPTER TWO

INNOVATING OUR PERCEPTION

One of the greatest gifts in my time working with The Body Shop was meeting Nykeba King, the woman who would eventually become the global director of inclusion, belonging, and well-being for The Body Shop. When we met, Nykeba was a regional coordinator who had been a store manager in Florida for more than ten years. She had an extraordinary talent for being able to adopt multiple perspectives in ways that provided paths forward and paths toward action that other people often could not see.

Nykeba had an immense talent for communicating with the entire organization as they considered this big shift in policy. The Body Shop was extremely committed to the vision of Inclusive Hiring, but there were, of course, a large number of practical concerns that the stores needed to navigate. Nykeba was especially proficient when it came to honoring the internal shift it would take the team to make to create the big transformational opportunities SuperLoop Praxis would bring to The Body Shop. Nykeba's ability to engage with the perceptions at each level of the I/WE/ALL was instrumental to the success of her company's cultural reinvigoration. She knew how to communicate the strategic level of the ALL to those who reported to her, and she was incredibly capable of consistently communicating concerns and progress to the executive team. She, most importantly, used her ability to inhabit other perspectives to practice Actionable Awareness, resulting in practical steps like crafting educational materials and instituting cohesive learning experiences throughout the entire organization of five thousand team members.

Nykeba's actions are an ideal demonstration of the SuperLoop Praxis. Operating within the SuperLoop Praxis model means that we have the opportunity to transform our perceptions with a number of goals in mind—owning our beliefs rather than them owning us, being responsible for our thoughts and how they influence our behaviors toward others, and being aware that the realities of others will be based on their individual perceptions. An awareness of our surroundings and our own thoughts creates the ability to have a high level of influence on how we perceive our daily reality, and changing the way we perceive our reality unlocks the ability to overcome problems that previously seemed insurmountable, or even those that were completely hidden from view.

Nykeba's particular skill for engaging with the I/WE/ALL became critical for The Body Shop and its transition to a new hiring and recruitment model. Her role in their transformation led to her becoming the global director of inclusion, belonging, and well-being. These skills she chose to deepen as she grew her own leadership were absolutely critical for an organization committed to being good humans while creating a good business.

Engaging with Perception for Organizational Transformation

There are numerous benefits to measuring and engaging with perception throughout our operations across the I/WE/ALL of an organization.

Examining these questions with a clear mind and a fresh perspective allows for flexibility, innovation, and adaptation at all levels. A lack of clear perspective results in living and engaging through assumptions—assumptions that are based on your personal experiences rather than those of the other person. Rather than mining for new solutions, a company continues "doing what they've always done." An organization that refuses to see when it needs to adapt often finds itself on the chopping block and in a maladaptive state once the world has changed enough around them.

Nykeba's abilities come from a long line of perspective-based innovators. There are numerous examples of organizations utilizing a clear perspective of the I/WE/ALL to their great benefit. In 1997, Apple questioned the ALL-level perception that it should offer a wide array of merchandise, saving the company when it shrank down to selling only computers, phones, and musical devices after decades of striving toward selling dozens and dozens of unpopular peripherals.[20] To achieve this, they needed to remake their organizational development practices and processes, as well as to create team buy-in to focus on their core products. This necessitated reframing their perspective for teams and individuals to meet the needs of the ALL.

In 2010, Zappos changed from a pure merchandise-delivery service to an experience that emphasized amazing customer service,

---

20   Walter Isaacson, *Steve Jobs* (Abacus, 2015).

which placed them at the forefront of online sales.[21] They Operationalized this by allowing untimed calls and allowing service representatives to engage in duties outside of the standard conception of their roles—such as ordering on behalf of a caller or even directing customers to other services when needed. In 2008, because of the challenges they faced in the economic downturn of the Wall Street crisis, Starbucks found innovation by questioning the internal perception that they should be a company of constant growth and physical expansion. After careful examination of their strategic plans and the accompanying sense of identity, they were able to save the company by shrinking the number of locations, closing 977 of them. Instead of stressing growth over all things, they centralized emphasis to the customer experience at individual stores.[22] To centralize customer interactions, they needed to retrain their employees and redesign their stores to do the same.

All of these businesses questioned what had become generally accepted internal perceptions, the sentiment that the current state of things is correct because "this is what we've always done" as well as "this is what our industry has always done." To survive these crises and prosper, they needed to question themselves and think critically about their current context with a level of perception that took into account the I/WE/ALL levels of their organization. They needed to engage with the possibilities and possibilities mindset that encouraged them to change their skill sets, embrace discomfort, and continually acquire new tools to effectively take on challenges. Each of these companies could have rested on their long track records of success and expansion.

---

21 Frances Frei and Anne Merriss, *Uncommon Service: How to Win by Putting Customers at the Core of Your Business* (Cambridge: Harvard Business Review Press, 2012).

22 John Quelch, "How Starbucks' Growth Destroyed Brand Value," *Harvard Business Review*, July 23, 2014, https://hbr.org/2008/07/how-starbucks-growth-destroyed.

Most companies would be ill-positioned for questioning their own success, but these companies were willing to continually reevaluate what worked and what did not in the face of a changing world. Apple, Zappos, and Starbucks were dealing with the massive upheavals of their eras in the same way that we're dealing with major shifts in our workforce, with artificial intelligence, and with global economic uncertainty that still echoes from the COVID-19 pandemic of 2020.

The Body Shop, using SuperLoop Praxis, was able to harness an awareness of their own perception and the state of their I/WE/ALL—all while, perhaps most importantly, honoring and elevating the values the company holds at its core. They became pioneers of hiring and recruitment innovations while increasing their social impact results (the impact on various social groups like mothers returning to work, incarcerated individuals, etc.) by 300 percent. This is the process (and the results) of Operationalizing Consciousness—making our awareness of ourselves and others into processes and policies in an organization.

EQUITABLE AND INCLUSIVE HIRING

Employment is one of the great social and economic equalizers, and there are many factors that make it difficult for individuals (especially for system-impacted women and youths) to obtain employment. As a conscious organization, The Body Shop wanted to open employment up for populations historically overlooked in the hiring process.

To do this, they needed to question the common perceptions and practices surrounding hiring and employment. Who makes a good employee? How do we decide who to hire? Why do we require a GED, high school diploma, or college degree? What competencies do we actually need for employee effectiveness?

The commonly accepted paradigm for hiring is to find someone with a long work history, related experience and degree, and a skill set that closely matches the job in question. We do this by collecting a résumé and conducting interviews. Often this also includes referrals from related industries and people in our networks. Applicants are stratified based on their access to education. The now-outlawed practice of asking about previous income was another way of closing off hiring—ensuring that those who were already prospering and who fell into the preferred groups were the people who obtained a given position.

These traditional processes, of course, lock out anyone who falls outside of these groups. Being bound by the conventional perception of who makes an effective employee and which skills are valuable makes for a reality that is woefully shortsighted. Most people perceive this practice not as a choice they are making with their policies but as best practice in hiring. These perceptions are never questioned because they are deeply held on the I/WE/ALL levels of society. We have a perception of who is a professional, who is deserving of work, and who will be useful. None of these are objective realities, but they are rarely questioned. As I have learned, we miss out on a significant amount of innovation by not questioning these assumptions.

Left out of this system are parents who left the work market to raise their children (known as the motherhood penalty—although it could equally refer to any parent), those who didn't fit into the traditional education system, people who have entered the criminal justice system, and scores of others who don't fit into preconceived notions of hireability and professionalism because of assumptions about race, gender, class, and learning styles.

The people who are left out of these systems are presumed to not have transferable skills. A parent who temporarily left the workforce, in reality, has a huge variety of skills that are functional but are not recognized by the labor market. A parent needs to manage time, budget, delegate, outsource to professionals, manage timetables, schedules, and a thousand other activities that are planning-intensive, structured, and take years to learn inside of a professional organization. On top of this already-impressive range, parents must master the skills of executive function by managing their behavior and emotions to effectively lead their families. They're people who come with a huge suite of usable skills, but these skills don't translate into fitting our usual perceptions of professional skills, and so they are not identified and not taken into account during job searches or hiring. Despite these skills, women returning to the labor market after raising children tend to earn 33 percent less than their earnings prior to leaving the market.[23]

This isn't all that difficult for most to imagine, but let's challenge this perception further and reflect on those who are immediately disqualified from employment because of a criminal conviction. Don't many crimes involve ingenuity, planning, execution, leadership, and a recognition of opportunity and timing? A vast majority of criminal convictions are nonviolent, but all applicants with criminal histories are almost immediately ejected from the hiring process, making the market miss out on these skill sets. This belief was one of the primary assumptions that had to be questioned inside The Body Shop's equitable hiring program.

Questioning our perception of the hiring process, of applicants, and of the context we usually use during hiring opens up a whole new reality and a range of potentially valuable applicants. Something like car theft looks so concrete on paper, but the reality of such a thing shifts entirely when we challenge our perceptions. Why did that

---

23 "The Motherhood Penalty: Removing Workplace Barriers," Baker McKenzie, March 8, 2023, https://www.bakermckenzie.com/en/insight/publications/2023/03/the-motherhood-penalty-removing-workplace-barriers.

person commit that theft? What were the actual circumstances of the event? Was it an act of desperation based on circumstances? Was it an altruistic, risky action to feed their family because the person in question was stuck in a series of bad circumstances?

Questioning our perception unlocks a reality where this car theft might not be as concrete as we first thought. Why something was done is often as important as what was done. As it's described in the groundbreaking book *What Happened to You? Conversations on Trauma, Resilience, and Healing*, by Dr. Bruce Perry and Oprah Winfrey, it's the difference between asking, "What happened to you?" versus asking, "What's the matter with you?"[24]

We open up the opportunity for innovation and novelty when we allow ourselves to deviate from our assumptions and maintain a recognition that our perceptions are full of incomplete facts. Adam Grant writes about this in his pioneering book, *Think Again: The Power of Knowing What You Don't Know*: "Questioning our own perception is the key to transforming our lives."[25] Using our curiosity to seek out concrete information from multiple perspectives offers us an increased level of Actionable Awareness that opens up opportunities that are not available when we take societal assumptions at face value.

Take this further and consider the other realities our typical perceptions might block from us. What skills went into recognizing, stealing, and fencing that car? What kind of planning, initiative, improvisation, and monetization went into this car theft? What has this person learned from their experience inside the justice system that will serve them moving forward? What human experience do

24   Bruce D. Perry and Oprah Winfrey, *What Happened to You? Conversations on Trauma, Resilience, and Healing* (New York: Flatiron Books, 2021).

25   Adam Grant, *Think Again: The Power of Knowing What You Don't Know* (New York: Viking, 2021).

they have that the market might be missing? If we remove all the judgments that would typically surround such an act, isn't there an associated skill set that might be valuable to an organization?

The Perception Surrounding Inclusive and Equitable Hiring

The Body Shop engaged in questioning their fundamental perceptions on every level of their business (I/WE/ALL).

At the ALL level, they evaluated whether their current assumptions about their organization were serving their values and then asked whether there was a better set of beliefs and operating procedures to suit the realities of the hiring crisis, their renewal of their values, and the assumptions American (and global business) culture have about hiring and professional opportunities.

At the WE level, they evaluated how they were providing onboarding, orientation, and continued training at the team level in The Body Shop stores, warehouses, manufacturing houses, and management teams.

At the I level, The Body Shop questioned how they were individually supporting new and current team members in mastering and consistently developing the technical skills required to do their jobs effectively. They also questioned how they could provide material and social support for these employees by examining how transportation, continuing education, nutrition, mental health, and childcare needs would ensure that employees were set up for success, even adding a specialized position to help develop these elements.

The Body Shop wanted to reinvigorate their values while also addressing the hiring crisis experienced by most industries in 2019. It asked the following questions about the common perceptions surrounding hiring:

- Where should a company be recruiting new talent?

- Why do companies adhere to the typical process of looking at paper qualifications rather than looking at competencies, and how does this impact who gets an interview?

- How does the traditional/existing hiring model affect the I/WE/ALL of companies?

While engaging with SuperLoop Praxis, The Body Shop identified that institutions determine who they are with their perceptions and beliefs. They choose who to hire based on these same perceptions and beliefs, and these people ultimately make up a reality that endorses those unquestioned perceptions. One must change their perceptions to change who they are, and since The Body Shop wanted to shift their identity, they needed to shift their perceptions.

They did this by engaging with the Open and Inclusive Hiring model and seeking to hire individuals who are often left behind by traditional models. The Body Shop determined that an organization committed to equity must address a number of areas that are often neglected and unequitable by providing access to employment, one of the great economic equalizers. Companies stand to benefit greatly by not assuming that the skill sets of traditionally excluded individuals would not be valuable. The Body Shop utilized a competency-based approach to their hiring rather than the traditional metrics that were used to include or exclude individuals from the labor market.

A competency-based model represents a shift away from the hierarchical, nonequitable hiring model for, in this case, entry-level positions within an organization. The Body Shop did this by stripping away the typical hiring process and instead embracing a model that asked three simple questions that establish the physical ability to work inside the demands of a position and eligibility to work in the country in question:

- Are you eligible to work in the US (or relevant territory)?

- Can you lift more than fifty pounds?

- Can you stand for up to eight hours?

All other forms of screening and background checks were dropped. These simple questions established the ability and willingness to work rather than focusing on the individual's history and credentials. This enabled The Body Shop to concentrate on a competency-based model that could be used to identify and cultivate strengths in candidates rather than simply eliminating them from consideration based on their work history, education, or criminal record.

"THE COMPETENCY-BASED MODEL": A competency-based model of hiring and evaluation is focused on evaluating what an individual can do rather than an apparent academic, professional, or quantitative model that looks at traditional, hierarchical concepts. This model allows for including those who fall out of the traditional industrial, educational, and social constructs we typically use to engage with professionals.

Beginning at the screening stage, a competency-based model emphasizes human potential and productivity rather than limiting ourselves to the above concepts. This concept honors and values lived experience and human willpower. Their capability matters more than their paperwork. It also requires a robust organizational and professional development system to ensure continued advancement.

This is a large shift away from the traditional methodology of hiring, but when a person, organization, and culture work to shift their perceptions, their reality also changes. This shift manifested to great effect, beating the current market and putting The Body Shop in a better position than its competition, who could not find applicants for their open entry-level positions.

This large change wasn't without concerns from the employees at The Body Shop. This had to be addressed since any transformation requires buy-in at every level of the I/WE/ALL if it is to be successful. Nykeba was relentless in influencing Nicolas Debray, president of the Americas at The Body Shop, to commission an entire Inclusive Hiring strategic plan that was completed by G3. This work began with the Equity Audit to ensure that, from the very beginning, all levels of voices were included in identifying gaps and strengths. Following the completion of the plan, a summary was shared as The Body Shop sent communications, held town hall forums, committed to upskilling the current team members in the entire enterprise, and outlined the specifics of the strategy and the particulars of the new Inclusive Hiring process. The Equity Audit specifically identified gaps in retention and hiring, as well as gaps in conflict resolution and communication. The Inclusive Hiring initiative was the perfect opportunity to engage in these gaps.

The Body Shop also invested in training store managers to engage in conversations surrounding Inclusive Hiring. This is where the talents of SuperLoop-trained employees truly came into play. The retail and middle management had a number of questions that amounted to pushback against the implementation of Inclusive Hiring—"What if these new hires are hardened criminals?" "What if they don't have the education to work with us?" "What if my other team members do not feel safe working with this population?"

In response to this, G3 worked to create clarity and share their perceptions and facts surrounding the program. The management team at The Body Shop implemented organization-wide G3-led learning labs that provided a chance to shift perspectives surrounding these issues.

First, employees were asked to voice their concerns. In the case of Inclusive Hiring, these concerns involved not knowing what past history the new employees might have—Were they criminals? Could they be trusted?

In response, employees were asked a number of questions meant to offer an opening to expand their perceptions (and therefore their reality), including the following: Have you ever been arrested? Has anyone in your family been arrested after a wild night? Could that have turned out to be much more serious if the circumstances were slightly different? Do you know/are you related to felons? Have you or anyone you know ever been less than fully honest on a legal document? Have you ever been close to not paying your bills? Have you ever been uninsured?

By the conclusion of these inquiries, a realization came over the group—they were ultimately not very different from the people who would be hired. In fact, this endeavor was not about hiring people who were different from the current employees, but rather people who had been subject to the same systems and realities. This process also brought to light unconscious biases that we all hold at various levels and how these inform our perspective and ultimately how we do or do not create inclusion and belonging. This is the legacy of the core values Dame Anita left them all "to create a fairer and more beautiful world." Adhering to their commitment to transparency, G3 and the leadership were very clear and honest about the realities of this program and its implications, both challenges and opportunities.

HUMAN VIBE: "CLARITY CREATES BUY-IN." In order to have true buy-in to a concept, the I/WE/ALL must be conveyed with a clear and transparent dialogue. This process begins with communicating the context surrounding the habits in the workplace practice. Team members should be informed of the strategy, both operational and financial impact, and processes involved. This is best facilitated by the SuperLoop practices of FeedForward and Authentic Communication. In the case of The Body Shop, it also involved modeling the entire process through role practice. In this exercise, one employee took on the role of an employee at The Body Shop and another acted as a customer while an observer watched the interaction to provide feedback to both on their conversations, talking points, and potential obstacles they may face.

AUTHENTIC COMMUNICATION

Authentic Communication involves being open and honest and making data statements with your communication. It involves dispelling Artificial Harmony and engaging with others with the I/WE/ALL in mind. Authentic Communication uses the "Curious Question" and "Call Forward" models described in chapter 2. It is a mutually beneficial process with the foundations of Generous Listening that fosters the ability to be in integrity with oneself while creating the space for others to show up authentically.

AUTHENTIC COMMUNICATION

The process of engaging with an individual directly with the belief that their commitment is to be the highest and best version of themselves and in a neutral fashion, creates the space for us all to show up in new ways. An invitation to connect for quick feedback and exchanges of perspective without completing the entire FeedForward process.

Finally, the process within SuperLoop Praxis for reaffirming the organization's values in these learning labs involved reflecting upon the mission of The Body Shop—to increase equity for all groups, especially for system-impacted populations. The US has the largest number of incarcerated individuals on Earth, housing 20 percent of the world's incarcerated people.[26] According to some sources, one in four Black men will be incarcerated in their lifetime (with only one in twenty-three white men incarcerated in their lifetime).[27] Incarcerated individuals have great difficulty finding employment, which can contribute to recidivism.

Some of the greatest difficulties to be found in the lives of those who are seeking to reenter society after time in the criminal justice system come in the form of a single question: "Have you ever been arrested for or convicted of a felony?" This question might immediately disqualify a candidate. At the very least, it almost certainly triggers unconscious bias in a hiring team. If you were a hiring manager who had the choice of interviewing a candidate with no

---

26   "Mass Incarceration: The Whole Pie 2022," Prison Policy Initiative, March 14, 2022, https://www.prisonpolicy.org/reports/pie2022.html.

27   Leah Wang, "Updated Data and Charts: Incarceration Stats by Race, Ethnicity, and Gender for All 50 States and D.C.," Prison Policy Initiative, September 27, 2023, https://www.prisonpolicy.org/blog/2023/09/27/updated_race_data/.

arrest record or one who has checked that box, who would you be most likely to choose?

The cycle created by the criminal justice system and mass incarceration reflects the inequalities of the larger culture, so addressing this inequality would make great strides toward achieving The Body Shop's mission of increasing equity through commerce.

An additional process G3 undertook was to ensure that the stakeholders of The Body Shop were able to engage in clear communication with the organization. The clarity aimed at the internal elements of the organization was also aimed outward. The Inclusive Hiring process was linked clearly to the long-term strategy of The Body Shop, the material benefits were documented, and the connection to the company values were well documented for any stakeholder who had questions. Rather than taking a reactive stance, The Body Shop proactively reached out to their stakeholders with clarity and engaged them in the same processes in which they opened communication with their employees.

The employees and stakeholders at The Body Shop were included in the strategy and values of the process, which led to dramatic, lasting transformation.

REGENERATIVE TRANSFORMATION

By 2020, The Body Shop had hired one thousand employees through the SuperLoop-Praxis-based Inclusive Hiring program. This endeavor was a large shift away from the traditional perception and reality of hiring, but when a person, organization, and culture work to shift their perceptions, their reality also changes. This shift manifested to great effect, beating the current hiring market and putting The Body Shop in a better position than their competition, who were consistently struggling to find applicants for their open entry-level positions.

In past years, not only did they internalize a recruiting team, but they also hired two additional recruiting consulting firms to fill positions. In 2022, two years after the launch of their successful program, the wider market still had 28 percent of retail positions unfilled. Even as the retail market recovered in the following years, The Body Shop kept a tangible lead on their competitors by having a more well-established workforce with less turnover than others in the industry.

This shift was life-changing for a number of people who would not traditionally be perceived to be desirable applicants. According to internal information gathered by an outside evaluator, Aperio Philanthropy, the newly hired Body Shop team members stayed employed, prospered in their roles, and generally experienced increases in satisfaction and positive perception of The Body Shop and their role there.

Approximately 150 of the new hires in both the retail and warehouse divisions were surveyed. Almost 50 percent of the surveyed applicants were unemployed at the time of their hire, and almost 20 percent of them had been unemployed for five months or more. Among all the respondents in the retail division, 48 percent of the new hires had previously been unable to find work that allowed them to work more than thirty hours a week. Eighty percent of those surveyed believed their new position at The Body Shop would lead to more opportunity. Twenty-one percent believed they would not have found other employment if not for Inclusive Hiring.

Approximately 50 percent of the respondents interviewed by Aperion indicated that they had faced a barrier to employment prior to being hired by The Body Shop—a lack of work experience, age discrimination, a perceived lack of education, an arrest record, an inability to interview effectively (or craft a résumé), or discrimination based on their ethnic background. One-quarter of the interviewees indicated that they had applied to The Body Shop specifically because of the Inclusive Hiring process.

To top all of this off, the respondents to Aperion's survey indicated that they had grown in their executive function and smart skills, including:

- communication

- collaboration

- time management

- stress management

- conflict resolution

Finally, a majority of respondents indicated an improved confidence regarding their personal and professional abilities, potential future job performance, and ability to find future work. The respondents also indicated a high level of trust in The Body Shop as an employer, with retail rating it four and a half out of five and the distribution division rating it four out of five.

The Impact of Equitable and Inclusive Hiring

This process empowered the I/WE/ALL of The Body Shop by Operationalizing their high drive to be an equitable company. As part of their Inclusive Hiring drive, they exceeded their annual strategic KPIs by drastically increasing their retention. They made a measurable difference in the lives of new team members, and they created stronger teams by improving their embodiment and practices of their culture of equity by changing their perception—which then changed their reality, resulting in achieving performance outcomes for the ALL.

This program initially began in 2019 in the United States, then expanded across North America and the United Kingdom. The Body

Shop then implemented the program across Australia and Brazil. In her role as the global director of inclusion, belonging, and well-being, Nykeba led this effort to engage in open and equitable hiring while deconstructing unconscious bias with new upskilling for the entire Body Shop community.

Perception isn't just a force that influences our cultural norms surrounding hiring and employment; it's also a force that sets our expectations of leadership, our ideas about problem-solving, and the way we conduct ourselves socially and professionally. When The Body Shop began Operationalizing practices in line with their perception of their own company, they made it a reality—and this brought their values to life in the world with revolutionary results.

This transformation is possible for any company that is willing to examine the frame of perception that operates across the individual, team, and organizational levels. It allows for innovation and reinvention while also offering the opportunity to clear obstacles to productivity and communication in ways that traditional hierarchies cannot. These systems only become more powerful as we examine them alongside the second phase of SuperLoop Praxis—the way our leadership and teamwork are affected by neurobiology and the teamwork techniques we will cover in the next chapter.

"If I can't do something for the public good, what the hell am I doing?"

—DAME ANITA RODDICK

"Not everything that is faced can be changed,
but nothing can be changed until it is faced."

—JAMES BALDWIN[28]

CHAPTER THREE

SUPERLOOP

On a beautiful San Diego morning in 2016, I found myself in a conference room leading the annual strategic planning meeting alongside The Chopra Center's executive and senior leadership team. The center had been training with SuperLoop for more than fifteen months with the goal of empowering their employees with communication tools, accountability, and conflict resolution competencies to increase their global commitment to elevating well-being. The first day's session was focused on CliftonStrengths-Based Leadership, a development program that helps employees identify and leverage their individual strengths to enhance their performance across their personal and professional lives. This was training that would begin to inform how the leadership team would be committing to their

---

28   James Baldwin and Randall Kenan, *The Cross of Redemption: Uncollected Writings* (New York: Pantheon Books, 2010).

strategic priorities for the next year while creating a new common language.

The conference room was gorgeous, with a rustic fireplace and the smell of breakfast foods wafting through the entirety of the meeting hall. The clear light of Southern California streamed through the windows and caught on the slick graphics The Chopra Center had created especially for this meeting. This three-day strategic planning meeting was the culmination of a lot of work on the parts of both the G3 and the Chopra teams. They had participated in an Equity Audit of their company—an evaluation of their leadership practices and each division's systems and processes. They'd worked hard to address the fact that their organization had identified gaps in their accountability and that they were inconsistent in achieving their annual KPIs. Today was the day they were going to review those results and create their strategic plan for the next year. They were, at this point, a $20 million company celebrating their twentieth year in service to the world. This was a day that was serving as the culmination of a lot of history and a lot of work, so much was riding on the outcome of this meeting.

I was in a familiar place; most of the teams I have worked with over the past thirty-five years have met me in this conference room atmosphere. But despite the familiarity, the sunlight, the ayurvedic candles I always light for workshops, and the normally open and welcoming, holistic demeanor of The Chopra Center and its leadership, the vibe in the room was off that day.

This was November 8, the day after the 2016 election in the United States that placed Donald Trump as the president, a defeat for the Democratic candidate of Hillary Clinton. This was a particularly fraught time for the leadership of this company, which was largely made up of moderate and progressively aligned people. As the meeting was about to begin, I noticed small clusters of people congregating, some of them weeping (which wasn't odd given the heart-centered nature of The Chopra Center—remember, perception is reality, and this open expression is something the I/WE/ALL of the center embraced and practiced). The room was filled with emotions alongside a great deal of enthusiasm for the big day we had in store. I began to calculate how the intensity of the political and energetic state around us was going to impact our session.

We kicked off the meeting, and one of the chief executives, Krista, took the floor and opened our workshop—but things didn't quite go to plan. Krista was distraught about the state of the country, and true to the high-harmony nature of The Chopra Center, she was sensitive to the high emotions being expressed by her team and wanted to acknowledge it. Krista discussed her hopes and fears about the future and the impact it was clearly having on her and the team. She stood in front of the senior leadership who had assembled for the sessions and poured her heart out for almost forty minutes. Her altruistic intention was to support her Chopra community.

It was intense and engaging, and the room was genuinely moved by her bravery in communicating her feelings and acknowledging theirs. That day, however, had been rigorously scheduled. When Krista had finished, she realized that the entire endeavor would now be way beyond the scheduled end time for the first activity of the day. She was flustered, and, glancing down at the agenda, she made the executive decision to scrub the first part of the session, where the leadership (each person at the session) was prepared to present their prework. Discussing What's Working and What's Not Working (W4) within The Chopra Center was to be an absolutely critical moment and an act of courage for everyone involved. This evaluation method is a chance to honor one's own voice and the voice of their organization by way of evaluating how that voice is actually showing up in action.

The ability to openly communicate what is not working was especially challenging in the high-relational, high-well-being environment that did not easily express what may be perceived as negative. In general, the Chopra team was struggling with Operationalizing the practice of Healthy Conflict and was experiencing Artificial Harmony. Not having the ability to openly discuss challenges was getting in the way of team members' and the business's ability to create innovations to further honor the mission and values they had pioneered in the industry.

As part of facilitating courses in SuperLoop Praxis, G3 designates team members who serve as Vibe Guides, individuals who use our practices on communication and accountability to coach in real time to ensure that clear and aligned communication is being practiced. I was the Vibe Guide for the room on this day. We call this framework Humancentric Facilitation, a methodology that is focused not only on acknowledging strengths and increasing various competencies but also on discovering our blind spots as individuals, teams, and the organization in real time.

I looked around the room, gauging the vibe coming from the team, and I noticed that there were some distinct signs of discomfort. People were shifting in their seats, their arms crossed, looking at each other for support, eye-rolling, yet relying on body language instead of actually speaking. The team members were clearly experiencing distress, yet the leader did not notice, and more importantly, no one in the room prioritized acknowledging it. They were clearly uncomfortable, but Krista was focused on keeping the day on track and was distracted by her own personal discomfort and the disequilibrium in the team. She, therefore, was not seeing what I was observing.

I knew that, despite her calm exterior, Krista was experiencing a state known as amygdala hijack, a neurological state that impairs the ability of a person who is experiencing strong emotion to access their executive function or regulate their autonomic nervous system. She was unable to engage with the situation around her because her biology had taken over and was actively interfering with her higher brain function.

This was a huge teachable moment and one that very much illustrated the concepts The Chopra Center had been working on for months. So I interrupted the meeting—and I began the steps that would empower them in the practice of engaging in Actionable Awareness and dispelling Artificial Harmony.

SuperLoop and the Systems That Drive Us

Although this social dynamic of avoiding uncomfortable situations might sound familiar or even simple, interrupting it and instead engaging with people openly, honestly, and effectively requires that we become aware of a number of factors that drive our communication, our relationship with conflict, and how we perceive the world.

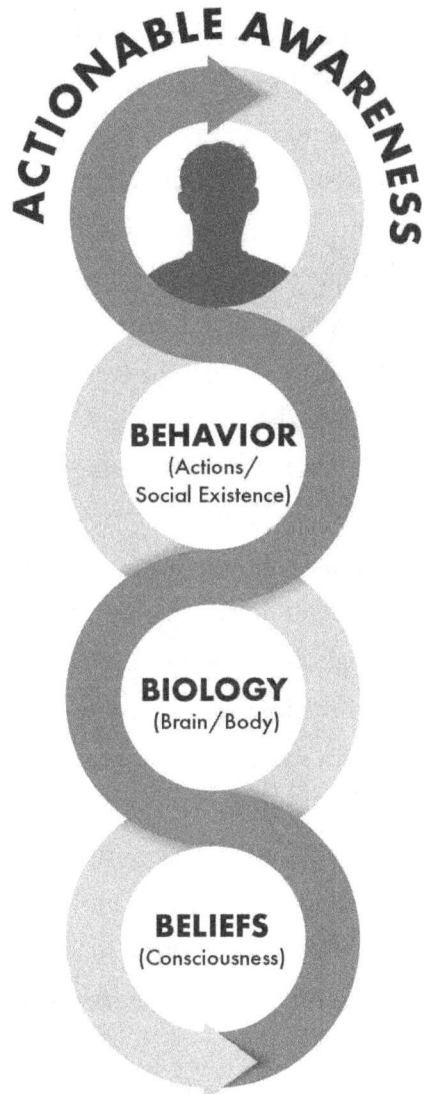

ACTIONABLE AWARENESS

BEHAVIOR
(Actions/
Social Existence)

BIOLOGY
(Brain/Body)

BELIEFS
(Consciousness)

Nobel Peace Prize winner Daniel Kahneman wrote about the way we process the world when we encounter perceived conflict in *Thinking, Fast and Slow*. In this book, Kahneman identifies two intermeshed systems we use to manage stress in our experiences. He identifies these as Systems 1 and 2.[29]

System 1 is our system for intuition. It operates automatically and without being in our voluntary control. It's responsible for instantaneous decisions we make without even realizing we're making them. These include recognizing objects, associating sound with meaning, and making snap judgments associated with emotion about a person or situation. Kahneman writes that System 1 relies on heuristics, mental shortcuts that can be efficient—but which can also lead us to make errors in judgment by engaging in cognitive bias. This system can be easily influenced by our experiences and becomes a source of intuitive judgment (for better or for worse influencing our beliefs about the future).

Kahneman describes System 2 (which runs simultaneously to System 1) as our more deliberative thinking system. It is slower, more contemplative, analytical and (most importantly) conscious. Mental activities that require effort belong in System 2: strategy, logical reasoning, solving complex problems, deciding what to do in the face of contrasting evidence. System 2 activities are associated with self-control, critical thinking, logical reasoning, and conscious deliberation.

As we've previously explored, perception is reality, and our perception begins with our processing and with the body (a construct that is often referred to as "the mindbody"). The first step to understanding how we engage with conflict and tension is to understand

---

29   Daniel Kahneman, *Thinking, Fast and Slow* (New York: Farrar, Straus, and Giroux, 2011).

the biological processes that are activated when we experience tension, stress, or apparently threatening situations. These biological processes further impact our beliefs and behavior, and this creates a positive feedback loop (the scientific term for a self-reinforcing cycle). This loop reinforces both the biology and thinking that influence our behavior and then, by amplifying the motivating factors, reinforces the behavior itself. This is a process we are not generally aware of, but it has a massive impact on how we handle stress and conflict.

As complex as our consciousness is, that complexity is, at times, exceeded on the biological level. It's not a mystery to anyone reading this that our brains are an incredibly complex system. It's made up of interconnected regions that are responsible for various functions. As people in charge of organizations where conflict and stress must be managed, the regions of chief interest to us are the prefrontal cortex and the amygdala.

The amygdala is a small, almond-shaped structure that is a key component in our limbic system (the system that governs the behavior and functions we need for survival). The amygdala plays a critical role in processing fear and aggression. It also plays a critical role in our survival instincts. Generally, we make rational decisions with a region of our brain called the prefrontal cortex.[30] This is the part of our brain function that we are most aware of, but it is far from the only structure at work when we engage with the world. What appears to be a purely rational decision has many processes at work that make our decisions and reactions much more complex than they initially appear to be. When we experience stress, we have a biological reaction to it. Any

---

30   Mark G. Baxter and Paula L. Croxson, "Facing the Role of the Amygdala in Emotional Information Processing," *Proceedings of the National Academy of Sciences* 109, no. 52 (2012): 21180-1, https://doi.org/10.1073/pnas.1219167110.

stressful experience, *real or perceived*, that is interpreted as a threat activates the fight-or-flight reaction from the amygdala.

DEFENSE RESPONSES	SURVIVAL BEHAVIORS
Fight	Looking good
Flight	Being right
Freeze	Being in control
Diassociate	Avoidance of conflict
Appease	Keeping small

Although fight-or-flight is the terminology typically used to describe these states, human beings actually react in a variety of ways to amygdala hijack; they fight, flight, freeze, dissociate, or appease (which is sometimes referred to as fawning). An FFFDA reaction is an effort to end the perceived danger of a stressful situation by the means they've been conditioned to believe is most effective. The SuperLoop of their beliefs, biology, and behavior is the reactive strategy they utilize to navigate stress and is thus the way they've learned to cope with an FFFDA scenario. The survival behaviors listed above are interchangeable responses in the FFFDA response, as they show up differently for each person based on their own history.

Let's visualize this in a professional context: An individual who has had a series of aggressive supervisors, for instance, might have learned to agree with everything they're told to avoid stressful interactions—this would be a combination of disassociating and appeasing. The amygdala regulates the release of stress hormones like cortisol and adrenaline and our parasympathetic nervous system, which regulates our heart rate and our breathing.[31] This response is generally automatic and occurs before our conscious mind even has a chance to comprehend the reality of a given situation.

This was undoubtedly very handy in the early days of humanity when we might find ourselves being chased by a sabertooth tiger. The amygdala activates the processes that release cortisol and adrenaline, which causes our parasympathetic nervous system to become more active. Our heart beats faster, our sensory processing becomes more acute, and we're primed for action. It's a marvelous system that yields marvelous results—when it's needed.[32]

Unfortunately, we rarely need an adrenaline rush during a meeting. Perhaps even more unfortunate, this lack of needing an adrenaline rush rarely keeps us from getting into a state of amygdala hijack. This is because our biology cannot differentiate between an actual threat and a perceived threat—and the situations that we perceive to be a threat will vary wildly depending upon our past conditioning, our frame of mind, and the context of a situation.

When our biology enters a state of amygdala hijack, our actions will make sense to us—we'll be reacting to a perceived threat—but these same actions are not understood by someone who is not living inside of our perception and our body. They have not had our lived

---

31   Sourya Acharya and Samarth Shukla, "Mirror Neurons: Enigma of the Metaphysical Modular Brain," *Journal of Natural Science, Biology, and Medicine* 3, no. 2 (2012): 118–124, https://www.ncbi.nlm.nih.gov/pmc/articles/PMC3510904/.

32   Earl K. Miller, David J. Freedman, and Jonathan D. Wallis, "The Prefrontal Cortex: Categories, Concepts, and Cognition," *Philosophical Transactions of the Royal Society of London. Series B, Biological Sciences* 357, no. 1424 (2002): 1123–1136, https://doi. org/10.1098/rstb.2002.1099.

experience and do not have the same conditioning we've received from our childhood, our past trauma, and our social conditioning, so their actions will appear to be motivated by different factors than they actually are. We might perceive a person undergoing amygdala hijack as aggressive, frantic, or angry even as they're actually trying to navigate what is a survival response. Think about it this way: our mindbody reacts to perceived stress as if our leader or coworker (or life partner, children, parents, neighbor, etc.) is that aforementioned sabertooth tiger. This freezing, fighting, or dissociation is all a result of the same systems at work despite potentially looking very different.

But the impact of the amygdala hijack doesn't end in that moment. It impacts the way we react to future phenomena by teaching us that our FFFDA response is a good way to navigate those challenging experiences. That amygdala hijack behavior becomes more and more embedded, and voila! We have created the new normal without even knowing it. The implications of creating FFFDA as our normal state impact all our relationships and our health biomarkers.

This state of struggle is so constant for us that it has entered quite a bit of religious and philosophical discussion throughout human history. The mystics use terms such as grasping, attachment, craving, avidya, and clinging to name this state. These terms describe the psychological and emotional patterns that trap us in the cycle of desire, dissatisfaction, and suffering. When this is our default existence, our mindbody becomes more comfortable in a chronic state of dysfunction than being in a consistent state of homeostasis—stability and balance—in the face of changing external conditions. The good news is we have all the proper hardware and software to evolve this pattern.

We, as humans, are not fully beholden to our amygdala-driven reactions to what happens to us. We have another structure, a structure known as the prefrontal cortex, that houses much of our conscious thought. This is the region of our brain where we mediate and navigate our behavior. The amygdala and similar structures are in constant communication and negotiation with our higher functions. This constant ebb and flow is a concept that G3 has dubbed as the SuperLoop.

"SAYING THE UNSAID": Much of what hampers our communication (and therefore our perception and our reality) is that we do not Say the Unsaid. We are frequently aware of subtext, tension, or other important, material facts that we do not address because we have been socially conditioned to remain mute in the face of the power hierarchies we were brought up in. This conditioning also limits our competency in communicating what may be perceived as critical or unpopular, therefore creating environments of Artificial Harmony rather than a place to practice Healthy Conflict.

Making a sustained, directed practice of Saying the Unsaid is the foundation of transparency. It creates authenticity and improves an organization's competencies in communication, productivity, and morale. Saying the Unsaid requires an Actionable Awareness of our intended message and how that message will be received by the individual or team with whom we are communicating. It requires a change in our perceptions of hierarchy because an individual needs to be able to speak honestly and openly without the fear of ego-driven or status-based reprisals. This practice also demands an increased sense of personal responsibility because Saying the Unsaid requires the willingness to engage in difficult conversations that we instinctively try to avoid.

What the SuperLoop Looks Like in a Professional Setting

My experience at The Chopra Center was a clear encounter with someone having an amygdala hijack episode. Defining this experience in a scientific way makes it sound like a dramatic event, but it isn't. To a greater or lesser extent, these events happen every day. Consider the following hypothetical example that demonstrates some of the many ways that amygdala hijack might manifest in our behavior.

Paola, a junior partner, is late for a meeting with her supervisor. She has a reason for being late—her car inexplicably broke down on the way to work, and she needed to have it towed to safety. Each of these steps has activated her amygdala more and more. Her car breaking down is something she can easily afford to fix now, but in the past, this would have been economically devastating. She has recently been frustrated with some of her boss's leadership, but she doesn't know how to approach her concerns. Her career is extremely important to her on both an emotional and financial level, and she knows this job is unique and to some extent irreplaceable. Once she's in the Uber, Paola can't stop imagining what would happen if she were to lose her job (even though she's in no danger of *actually* losing her job—she's never late, and everyone has the occasional setback, like a car malfunction).

Consequently, Paola is highly agitated by the time she arrives at work. She is in a state of amygdala hijack. The next time she faces stress, her reaction is intense, overwhelming, and out of proportion to whatever triggers it. It happens when Paola's boss makes an offhand, joking comment when she walks in, and Paola responds intensely. Perhaps she blows up defensively, immediately pointing out a way that her coworker gets to regularly show up late without anyone ever commenting. Maybe she gets even more defensive, uttering a sarcastically edged response that points out that patriarchy has won once again. In a different situation, Paola might freeze, unable to respond, or she might break down crying and leave the room, unable to proceed with their check-in meeting. Can anyone relate? In my work, both internally in my teams and working in other companies, I have seen versions of this play out again and again.

These FFFDA responses are common ways we might see these states manifest in a workplace setting. Different people and circumstances lead to different responses, but the results are rarely beneficial in our everyday lives, as we are not *consciously responding* but are *unconsciously reacting* through the lens of our past conditioning. You have likely seen a coworker or direct report overreact, not react, or react strangely in a stressful situation. The hot-reacting peer or passive-aggressive coworker is a result of this SuperLoop in action.

Much of our biological response to stress comes from our past experiences. We're reacting to current phenomena with a biology that has been created by our past. This sounds complex, but in the same vein, few people would be surprised to learn that Paola had a strict parent who was quick to discipline her for the slightest infraction or that her parents didn't deal well with crises and created an unsafe environment for their children by overreacting strongly when things went wrong. Paola might also have encountered harsh discipline in school, have been raised in a culture that encouraged women to be submissive, or any number of other factors that built and reinforced this conditioning. Our experiences set up our biology, and our biology influences us long after we've stopped consciously thinking about the experiences of the past. That's the SuperLoop in action.

In our hypothetical, Paola learned early on (and throughout her life!) that events similar to this were uncomfortable, and her neurology became wired to compensate for this. She is what is commonly known as a people pleaser and avoids conflict by being a perfectionist who tries to maintain control of situations as much as possible. Paola unconsciously reacts in these ways to avoid situations that will bring her stress and pain. She typically goes along to get along to keep the peace in relationships.

Although this almost sounds like a disorder, this is all very natural—it is the way our nervous systems have evolved. We all engage in this process and grapple with these biological circumstances. Our nervous systems are excellent at avoiding pain and uncertainty, and many of our stress responses are meant to do exactly that—avoid pain and seek safety in the way that seems most effective. In our biology, we have a component known as mirror neurons that contribute to our inclination to avoid causing harm to others. These mirror neurons enable us to empathize with others to such an extent that we actually feel their pain as if it were our own.[33]

Read that last line again.

So as we grow in Actionable Awareness of ourselves, we recognize that the physical and emotional discomfort we experience as we perceive the pain of others is real. Maybe these situations are so difficult not only because we are not sure of exactly what to say but also because we think we are going to hurt another person and know that we will feel something similar to their pain—and so we seek to avoid it all together.

Which is where we come back to Paola.

Paola was unequipped to clear this misunderstanding *because* she was experiencing an amygdala hijack—and because she had not

33 Sourya Acharya and Samarth Shukla, "Mirror Neurons: Enigma of the Metaphysical Modular Brain," *Journal of Natural Science, Biology, and Medicine* 3, no. 2 (2012): 118–124, https://www.ncbi.nlm.nih.gov/pmc/articles/PMC3510904/.

learned to engage with her SuperLoop by interrupting the conscious and unconscious pattern of what was happening in her mindbody. She could not give a simple, reasonable explanation because her body and mind were stuck in survival mode, activating an FFFDA response. If we're unaware of it, the SuperLoop phenomenon will also impact similar scenarios in the future. After this day, Paola has reinforced a pattern of perception where she has reason to react to future similar events in a fight-or-flight fashion. She is now more likely to experience an amygdala hijack in similar circumstances, which quickly becomes a self-reinforcing cycle and, as cognitive neuroscientists say, "What fires together wires together." Our brains—or our synapsis connections, to be precise—are built by default or design; new pathways are built by both conscious repetition of effective actions or unconsciously reinforcing of responses that no longer serve us. The choice is ours.

In other words, are you using your brain, or is your brain using you?

This process, with education and practice, can be interrupted and managed on the individual level (I) and on the collective levels of WE and ALL—a process that SuperLoop Praxis calls Actionable Awareness.

HUMAN VIBE: "I AM NEVER UPSET FOR THE REASON I THINK." This Human Vibe reminds us that we are rarely actually upset about what seems to be the originator of stress. Rather, we are likely being influenced by our experiences, our biases, and our biology. When we account for the influence of these elements, we can pause (breathe) and move forward in awareness, finding a better path forward rather than giving into our initial sensations, feelings, or thoughts.

Engaging with the SuperLoop: Actionable Awareness for Individuals and Institutions

Training individuals to engage with the SuperLoop involves self-awareness and self-regulation. These are challenging skills to master—emotions and perceptions are biological responses that have evolved to be processed. They are signals from our mindbody that we have a need that must be addressed. This is as literal as touching something hot or cold and knowing when to move your hand. If these are not processed, they are inevitably repressed, avoided, displaced, and projected on others. Unidentified and unprocessed emotions come out as behaviors in other areas. Much of what we refer to as "acting out" is some displaced response erupting in an uncontrolled way.

It becomes the commitment of both individuals and organizations to take responsibility for identifying these patterns—and to be committed to the practice of interrupting, managing, or mitigating them. Bessel van der Kolk, one of the pioneers of trauma-informed work and the author of *The Body Keeps Score: Brain, Mind, and Body in the Healing of Trauma*, tells us, "Trauma comes back as a reaction, not a memory."[34]

PROCESSING EMOTIONS

Emotions are evolved responses that help our survival when they are processed effectively.

---

34   Bessel van der Kolk, *The Body Keeps Score: Brain, Mind, and Body in the Healing of Trauma* (New York: Penguin Books, 2015).

They are signs on a road alerting us to the conditions around us, noting that something in our environment needs to be experienced, processed, and catalogued. This is often as a result of previously experienced phenomena rather than necessarily relating to the present conditions surrounding us. Emotions are not right or wrong—they are information that needs to be interpreted. Since we are thinking creatures, we can use that information to move forward as whole humans rather than leaving our biological impulses and unresolved traumas to hijack us when we least expect it.

We deal with emotions as information on a constant basis. Consider the phrases "I have a gut feeling," "It doesn't sit right with me," or "I can feel it in my bones." The ability to recognize and interpret sensations and physical cues is called somatic awareness. We are all born with the ability to be highly connected to our bodies. That is why infants and toddlers are so present to their needs and ensuring all those around them are as well. As we grow, we are conditioned into social systems that benefit from us being more attached to social approval (think school systems, religious institutions and eventually the work environment) that benefit from us being less aware of our own individual needs and more in tune with the needs of the social group: external approval.

Critical to processing emotions effectively is the act of recapitulation. Recapitulation is a deliberate examination of the emotions we experienced in a given situation. To recapitulate, we must examine what we felt, why, and other times we may have experienced those sensations. A proper recapitulation and self-examination practice can have a cumulative effect on our behavior, enabling us to change and evolve deliberately rather than endlessly repeating the patterns of our past.

Recapitulation is a self-healing practice that cleanses our experiences—actually processes the emotions from a neutral place—as the witness of our own life. I use the practice of recapitulation at night as part of my emotional healing commitment to myself. It takes five to ten minutes to close my eyes and walk through my day, making note of the feelings and thoughts that occurred in various situations. "That was a really fun meeting with my peer. That conversation with Tami, though, was tough; I felt anxious and unprepared."

At times, if I feel I still have unresolved feelings or circumstances, I will commit to journaling about them either as part of my journaling practice in the morning or by adding it to a list of situations that I delve into more deeply. Once a month, on a Sunday morning, I explore what there is for me to own that will support me in moving through to new elevations of liberation. Journaling is another tool that supports us in understanding our own growth. I began journaling in second grade and have kept some form of journaling process my entire life. Once a year, I will take a few hours and read back to reflect on ways I previously looked at situations versus how I am processing life now. It's a great self-accountability tool.

So where might employees get the opportunity to engage in recapitulation? In employee resource groups, in peer organizations, or as part of guided, institutionalized reflection, mentorship, and even in counseling. Ultimately, these opportunities for recapitulation address the real need organizations have to handle these experiences before they result in the derailing of the culture through organizational processes or losses of efficiency and satisfaction.

If we choose not to prioritize the time to connect to our feelings, emotions, and needs, then they are not processed. Fully processing emotions is a personal responsibility, and it comes in the form of action. Not processing our emotions creates toxicity in our own being. These SuperLoop reactions become something we believe is an inherent part of our own well-being.

You've likely heard someone say, "That's just who I am," in response to having a temper, being anxious, or being jovial. The SuperLoop, after all, feels like it's on autopilot, which is true. Fortunately, however, this is an autopilot we can rewire—*consistent interruption of previous patterns while actively engaging in new behaviors actually rewires the structure of this very "autopilot" system.* This makes the SuperLoop something we can actively influence with our every behavior.

So guess what? You can teach an old dog new tricks.

An Actionable Awareness of our SuperLoops (which also means an awareness of the fact that we are constantly carrying our past around in our reactions) means that we no longer approach disagreements by asking the other party, "What's the matter with you?" We instead lean into asking Curious Questions and approach the situation with, "What happened to you?" This worldview, in addition to being accurate on a biological level, is a worldview that allows people to collaborate and understand, rather than just judge one another on reactive autopilot. It's also a level of self-awareness that allows people to experience their amygdala hijack moments as processes that can be observed and embraced rather than as intrinsic character traits that are "just who you are."

Instead, someone might ask themselves, "Why did those words from my coworker bother me so much? Where is my responsibility in this situation? Why did I give up my power by freezing—choosing to say or do nothing leaving me agitated and resentful? What will I do better next time? How can I use this situation to practice new behaviors?" This Actionable Awareness gives us the ability to work on parts of our behavior and character that are usually taken as unchangeable.

Often, when we face a high-stress situation, our reactions can feel involuntary. A knowledge of SuperLoop and an Actionable Awareness of why we seem to have certain reactions can remind us that we have power over how we meet the world. Our biology influences us, but it does not determine us—unless we let it—as so many of us have been conditioned to do.

One of the Human Vibes explains the importance of being proactive about mastering SuperLoop: "Trauma not transmuted is transferred." No sentiment, reaction, or feeling simply goes away if it is ignored, repressed, or not processed. Just as a soda bottle resting usually will not explode, once the environment becomes intense and agitated, what is inside explodes all over others, and usually in destructive ways. When we discover sources of stress, conflict, or tension, these situations and emotions must be investigated and cleared so that it does not simply leak out in some other unpredictable fashion. If we do not understand the learned experiences that have conditioned us to experience amygdala hijack, we'll never be able to control when these conditions emerge in other areas of our lives. This becomes particularly important for organizations because people who have mastered their inner lives with consistent mindfulness are more capable of engaging in Healthy Conflict, engaging in Authentic Communication, and Saying the Unsaid—all of which ultimately lead to greater employee well-being, satisfaction, and effectiveness.

AUTHENTIC COMMUNICATION SYSTEM

Generous Listening

Curious Questions

Responsible Responses

Call Forwards

Practice of
Healthy Conflict

— *Presenting Boundaries*
— *Saying the Unsaid*
— *Clearing Conversations*

FEED FORWARD

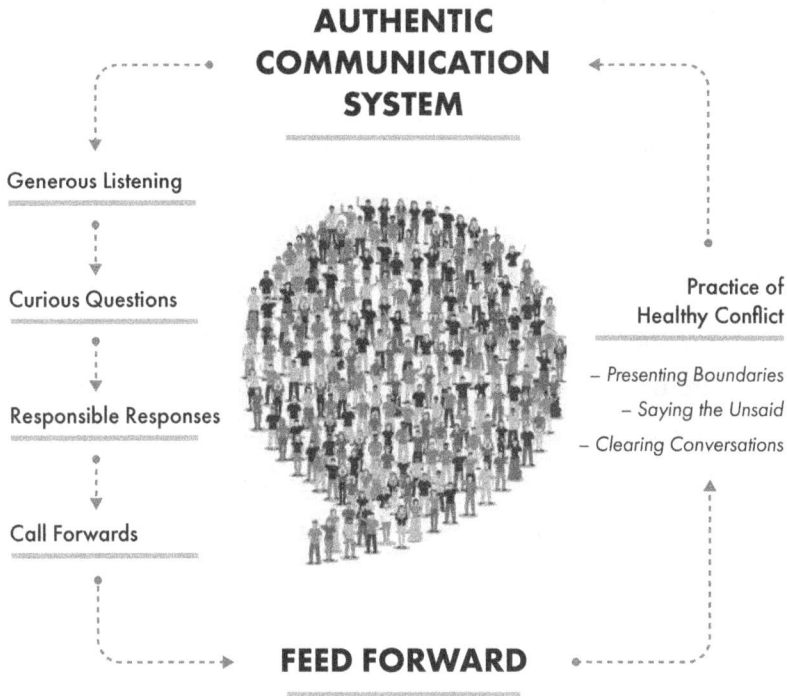

Emotions Are Evolved to Be Expressed

That day in The Chopra Center conference room, Krista was certainly in a state of amygdala hijack. Her SuperLoop was amplifying her discomfort at the massive and antagonistic change that had occurred in an election she was emotional about—and her SuperLoop made that situation run away from her. Since neither Krista nor the people in the conference room interrupted the process, the results were (at least initially) what Krista wanted from the situation.

I know I can relate to that. How about you? As a leader, when individuals and/or our teams are off, distracted, or hurting, we want to support them, to get them from discomfort to comfort. This instinct, however, can collectively take us off track when it comes to the ALL, the wider goals, the goals that do impact the individuals and the team as well as the entire system.

This is the kind of challenge every leader, and really every human being, works with as a professional—regardless of their background or of the context. Part of our functionality is to witness ourselves and to acknowledge where our feelings come from—and how they show up in our thinking and behaviors in ways that may or may not align with the kind of human and leader we are committed to being.

But there was a second complicating factor at work that day, one that challenged this situation for Krista and put an unfair level of pressure on her—a failure to Say the Unsaid by her team—and one that was reflective of a bigger, chronic problem that needed to be addressed. This ability, as we'll see, is absolutely critical to a healthy, successful organization—and the root of almost all the problems an otherwise healthy team experiences in their work culture.

"Between what is said and not meant, and what is meant and not said, most of love is lost."

—WIDELY ATTRIBUTED TO
POET KHALIL GIBRAN

CHAPTER FOUR

OPERATIONALIZING SUPERLOOP PRAXIS

O nce I'd stopped the meeting, I was determined to deepen the Humancentric Facilitation that we were undertaking, so I asked the room multiple times if anyone had anything they wanted to contribute.

"As the Vibe Guide, I want to stop here and check in. Would anyone like to Say the Unsaid and share what's going on for them?"

In this work, as team members learn new skills, silence and patience are some of the most valuable tools we practice—it's an action that involves being patient with the process as well as setting the new expectation of Authentic Communication.

"We're not doing what we have always done—moving on without the white elephant in the room being acknowledged. We are going to practice these new skills together."

Initially, everyone remained silent, and we sat in the San Diego sun as the entire team waited for someone else to break the silence.

So I waited. And waited. And I then invited participation at a new level. "I sense something is off here. Is anyone else getting that feeling?" Many people nodded their heads.

Finally, a brave masseuse, a person who was not even a member of the C-suite leadership (who might be more protected from a backlash caused by such an action), took the risk and raised her hand.

She acknowledged Krista for her inspiring comments and then, with clear apprehension, tentatively stated that the team had spent a significant amount of time preparing for today's discussion and that skipping over that to stay on schedule was disappointing and frustrating because it happened often.

I asked if anyone else felt that way. Again, as a group that was used to avoiding conflict and engaging in Artificial Harmony, the room was hesitant to acknowledge this. Then, slowly, one hand came up, followed by a half dozen, and then eventually more than three-quarters of the room had raised their hands to add their perspective and join the conversation.

Ultimately, most of the leadership of The Chopra Center had trepidations about already being off the meeting agenda. They wanted to engage with the work they'd prepared for that day and wanted to let their leader know that they disagreed with her choice to not discuss the prework, but nobody spoke up. The rest of the room had become too comfortable with their own frequent inaction and was prepared to allow the meeting to move forward just to avoid conflict and appease Krista for potentially both of their financial survival and the protection of their positional ego.

Krista, in a similar autopilot that manifested in a different way, had been too consumed by what was going on in her own mind and body to perceive this subtext and act on it. This was natural, and it was actually the initial impulse of a strong leader—she wanted to keep her team on track on this important day. I immediately wanted to interrupt the meeting to bridge the gap between Krista and her colleagues—but I held back.

Nobody was satisfied with the initial decision to move on in the day's agenda and skip the sessions they'd been working toward—yet all of them were willing to tolerate the all-too-familiar situation for the sake of what they believed to be team harmony. Human beings want to be polite, to not be hurtful, to support others. This can sometimes lead us to avoid conflict altogether even when it is critical to a team, relationship, or project. On top of this, their senior leader was lost in her own reaction to the trauma of the day, unable to gauge what her employees were not saying because she was locked into a state of overload.

Would you be surprised if I told you that 90 percent of the work I do with my clients involves an environment where the majority of the team members feel there is an obvious problem that isn't being addressed? This happens at all levels in the org chart. They'll know this is happening and can actually identify where the patterns of behavior are going to play out, yet they unconsciously (and sometimes consciously) respond with, "Well, that's not my problem," or, "I'm not sticking my neck out when nobody else will." I also hear, "I've tried to address it, but nobody listens," more times than I care to mention. The more convoluted and justified version I get is, "These are legacy issues, and they are a cultural problem that the executive team needs to handle."

My point is, just like the team watching Krista fall into an amygdala hijack on that day in The Chopra Center, our teams will often see a problem and then find a variety of reasons to avoid addressing it. The problem isn't usually that we don't know what to do—the problem is that we need to know and then act.

Leaders—take a beat and ponder. Does this sound familiar? Do you see people so swept up in their emotions or reactions that they do not accurately see the workplace around them? Do you see teams simply "go along to get along" and consequently have undesirable outcomes because of this unwillingness to engage in self-accountability and Peer-to-Peer Accountability? Have you struggled with your own leadership growth because you are counting on your team to Call you Forward, yet they don't?

Two powerful forces were at work that day, and they're forces that come to bear constantly in organizations that do not engage in Actionable Awareness on two fronts—management of the SuperLoop and Saying the Unsaid.

SuperLoop and Institutional Management

The training for mastering the SuperLoop involves engaging in role practice and ensuring that people (and institutions) are prepared for Vibe Guide direction of provocative conversations, conscious conflict, and Authentic Communication. The goal of these sessions is to provide practices that allow individuals to become more conscious of their SuperLoop and to thereby create an Actionable Awareness of themselves, and to ultimately provide a platform upon which we can cooperatively use this awareness to build new, more accountable cultural norms within an organization. The more aware we are, the greater our opportunity to engage with the world in a way that is conscious of how our own *beliefs and biology are driving our behaviors.*

The concept of Actionable Awareness applies to both the individual and organizational levels (the I/WE). We, in most of our interactions, engage in Artificial Harmony—the urge to avoid conflict despite the fact that this avoidance will ultimately be detrimental. This behavior causes us to avoid the reality that there is a subtext of tension and resentment that, if not addressed, will accumulate and blow like a shaken soda bottle.

ARTIFICIAL HARMONY

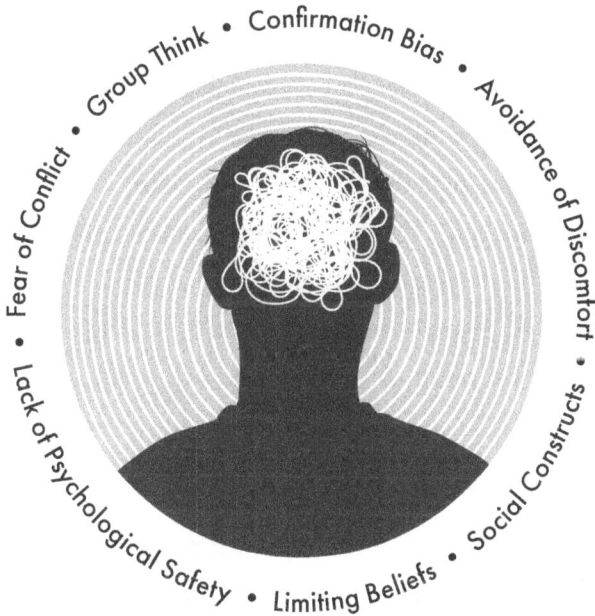

To illustrate and explore this, let's use a hypothetical situation involving a high-level senior leader named Marvin. Marvin has developed a pattern of arriving late to team meetings and not keeping similar commitments. One of the reasons that this pattern has persisted is the aforementioned tendency that organizations have to exist in Artificial Harmony. Marvin is a very well-liked employee. He keeps events lively and he's low stress to work with, so nobody wants to upset him. Furthermore, his cohort has decided that he "knows" that his lateness is a problem (after all, they've told him many times), and so they decided that they do not need to call attention to it.

ARTIFICIAL HARMONY

Artificial Harmony is when an individual chooses to "go along to get along." Although they know there are challenges in the system, they choose not to be responsible for addressing them. Often, this is because they do not want to be seen as a person who initiates conflict or who is not loyal to others, or they are a person who has been conditioned to be a people pleaser. People exist in Artificial Harmony because there are a number of benefits to not bringing challenges to light, including avoiding the perception of conflict, avoiding negative consequences, not having to inflict and/ or experience discomfort, and wanting to be seen as a team player.

Organizations, to their own detriment, tend to reinforce a state of Artificial Harmony for the sake of homogeny, Operationalized conformity, and for the sake of (what seems to be) stability. To add to this, there are a number of common factors that tend to reinforce Artificial Harmony. The first is that the hierarchical model tends to disallow Healthy Conflict, and mostly because they do not feel competent in giving, receiving, or addressing critical feedback. To add to this, direct reports who manage up to a supervisor in a traditional organizational structure have an internal fear of retaliation. This creates a situation where there is a valid fear of Healthy Conflict, so team members perpetuate Artificial Harmony for no other reason than as a perceived (or evidence-based) survival mechanism that has worked for them in the past.

It's easier to commiserate with the "here we go again" eye-rolling of our colleagues than to do something different. Because if we do something different, we are likely to be met with reproach from our cohort—there's the "Why did you bring that up? We all just want to get out of here so we can get some real work done" vibe that frequently comes into the narrative of those used to practicing Artificial Harmony. They are more interested in "going along to get along" rather than being the outlier who is owning their responsibility and being the one to behave in a new way. This takes courage; it's the more difficult short-term choice even though it leads to better results in the long term.

Companies also engage in operational choices that encourage Artificial Harmony. The choice to not create specific time in meeting agendas for Healthy Conflict is one that unconsciously Operationalizes Artificial Harmony by ensuring there is no designated space to practice Healthy Conflict. This means that confrontations, conflict, and respectfully disagreeing are not an operational priority specifically by not having an agreed-upon arena or procedure in which it is expected to occur, and this makes those that speak up perceived as an agitator or a rebel.

SAYING THE UNSAID

Much of what hampers our communication (and therefore our perception and our reality) is that we do not Say the Unsaid. We are frequently aware of subtext, tension, or other important, material facts that we do not address because we have been *socially conditioned* to remain mute in the face of the power hierarchies we were brought up in.

Making a sustained, directed practice of Saying the Unsaid normalizes authenticity and improves an organization's competencies in Healthy Conflict, communication, productivity, and its morale. It requires a change in our perceptions of hierarchy because individuals have a need for psychological safety, the belief that one will not be punished or humiliated for speaking up with ideas, questions, concerns, or mistakes while creating an environment where people feel comfortable taking personal risks by sharing thoughts and opinions and contributing to discussions without fear of negative consequences. This practice also demands an increased sense of personal responsibility because Saying the Unsaid requires the willingness to engage in difficult conversations that we instinctively try to leave as subtext. Saying the Unsaid requires an awareness of our intended message and how that message will be received. Saying the Unsaid is *not* permission to blame, shame, or manipulate others. Quite the contrary, it requires each of us to own our behavior in the current operational and cultural environment, to own how we have, by default or design, contributed to the outcomes, and to own that we are committed to doing differently moving ahead.

In SuperLoop Praxis, all meetings end with the agenda item of Saying the Unsaid. The purpose is to build a practice that creates two key outcomes:

1. Team members being responsible for contributing positive, negative, or unclear perspectives and engaging in Authentic Communication using those perspectives

2. The organization benefiting from the talent of all members by normalizing the practice of giving and receiving contrasting perspectives

Finally, Artificial Harmony persists because it seems easy. Healthy Conflict, on the other hand, takes significant energy and effort. If it's done right, it takes introspection, empathy, and efficient management. The easy path, unfortunately, is rarely the healthy path. Not brushing our teeth is also easy, but it inevitably has consequences. Artificial Harmony is similar. We reap the consequences if we don't engage in Healthy Conflict.

I constantly hear, "I'm really afraid about what will happen if I have this conversation."

To which I reply, "What does your life look like if you continue to avoid having that conversation? Fear those results, that abandoning of yourself, more than the results of one conversation."

There are seemingly small, rippling consequences that eventually become large when we practice Artificial Harmony. People want to be polite, they want to seem professional or compassionate, so they do not engage in calling Marvin forward, but instead leave this tension Unsaid. In our hypothetical situation, this means that Marvin cannot know how he's impacting others and the organization. As a result of this, projects will suffer, meetings will remain off-kilter, and, eventually, the ALL level of the company will be damaged—all because the

team is avoiding leaning into the situation to bypass their own discomfort and lack of acumen in a given situation. Artificial Harmony
is often a desire to avoid SuperLoop activation and discomfort, and so
we engage in it to keep the appearance of things running smoothly—
even when we all are aware on some level that it is not functional and
things are eventually going to fall apart.

The path toward dispelling Artificial Harmony necessitates
training and practice. Organizations engaging in the Operationalizing
Consciousness process begin this by using role practice to engage with
a recreation of circumstances that are creating strife in the organization. The SuperLoop practitioner creates a space where participants
are ready to bring forward the real situations that have remained as
unaddressed subtext and created unhealthy conflict.

In the case of our hypothetical example, Marvin's workplace
has experienced unresolved conflict and Artificial Harmony, so their
SuperLoop practitioner would engage in role practice with Marvin
and the employee who is willing to call Marvin forward. Through
this, the processes of Saying the Unsaid, engaging in Healthy Conflict,
and Calling Forward will enable this organization to engage with this
unhealthy conflict in a way that is productive, changes the pattern
for the future, and provides a new understanding and competencies
for everyone involved.

The conflict surrounding Marvin stems from the fact that he
tends to arrive late to important meetings. The SuperLoop facilitator,
at this point, will ask the participants about their reactions, assumptions, and how these elements might be conditioned responses from
their past and their social training.

Sharla, the team member who has presented this scenario with
Marvin, will have been asked by her SuperLoop facilitator to outline
the situation and then might be asked why she hasn't presented Marvin

with the pattern she's describing. Sharla says that she doesn't confront Marvin about these late arrivals because she can tell that Marvin gets upset when this is brought up. She knows Marvin cares about the team; however, she feels that Marvin's late arrivals represent a lack of care for the needs of everyone else involved in the meetings and that he's taking advantage of the fact that he's well-liked and charismatic. At this point, Sharla might be asked to provide a data statement about how these events impact her and the outcomes for the team:

"Marvin, when you arrive late, you throw off my next three meetings," or, "Marvin, when you arrive late, we're forced to rush important agenda items and we don't get important work done. Marvin, I am interested in how you would solve these issues, and when you are not here, we miss out on your strengths as a team."

Marvin, when he's confronted openly with these data statements and perspectives that have remained Unsaid, can now respond with full knowledge of the context. Now that the subtext of the situation has been spoken out loud, the issues can be confronted. Importantly, Marvin has an opportunity to provide key information—perhaps he takes extra care in preparing because of anxiety derived from his past or social conditioning. Perhaps growing up in a household that didn't stress deadlines but rather results, he didn't understand the impact on Sharla, who grew up in a very on-the-minute home. Now that Sharla has communicated, Marvin can dispel the notion that he doesn't value Sharla's time and plan for a future that involves both of their needs. This new knowledge provides Actionable Awareness for both Sharla and Marvin and a productive example for all on the team.

The Artificial Harmony that has delayed this conversation has been cleared (or the process of clearing this harmony has begun). Marvin and Sharla are no longer "going along to get along" but are rather openly and honestly dealing with each other. Marvin now has the opportunity to share his side of this conversation and to take responsibility for what he controls. Now Sharla no longer has to silently manage the fallout she and her team experience from late meetings.

With their SuperLoop training and role practice, Sharla and Marvin are instead engaging in a series of critical processes that make SuperLoop a workable model for individuals (and therefore benefit the institution). They are acknowledging the Artificial Harmony while practicing Saying the Unsaid, engaging in Healthy Conflict, Calling each other Forward, and having Clearing Conversations. Each of these concepts warrants further examination because each is a powerful tool in managing the forces that hamper organizations at every level.

Saying the Unsaid—the Quiet Part Loud

Part of engaging with the SuperLoop in healthy fashion involves practicing authenticity with both ourselves and those around us. This Actionable Awareness, starting with the decision to avoid Artificial Harmony by practicing Healthy Conflict, gives us the tools. Saying we want to avoid Artificial Harmony alone isn't enough. We also need to actively engage with the underlying tensions that make Artificial Harmony seem necessary in the first place. This, by necessity, involves engaging in Healthy Conflict, Calling our peers Forward, and asking Curious Questions.

So how does one practice Healthy Conflict? We've been trained to view the word "conflict" as a negative term. In reality, two worldviews are going to differ, and therefore, where they diverge, they may possibly find conflict. A traditional workplace likes to pretend that conflict does not exist. This isn't an attitude that solves issues but rather one that marginalizes ideas that fall outside the command-and-control ethic of an organization. Healthy Conflict allows for multiple viewpoints to be included and processed as part of a decision-making and resolution structure.

CURIOUS QUESTIONS

CURIOUS QUESTIONS

A tool that is used to create authentic listening. An individual utilizing curious questions will have an awareness of their biases going into communication. Curious Questions utilize curiosity that creates a space for deeper listening. Curious questions are collaborative instead of demanding a response. Curious questions are invitations to communicate that support all parties in being seen, felt, and heard. They are distinctly about non-judgement. Curious questions should involve a genuine desire for more information and an awareness that the individual making the inquiry is missing information and context. They are about solutions rather than about confirming one's judgment.

CALLING FORWARD

The process of engaging with an individual directly with the belief that their commitment is to be the highest and best version of themselves and in a neutral fashion, creates the space for us all to show up in new ways.

Calling Forward, the process of engaging with an individual directly with the belief that their commitment is to be the highest and best version of themselves aligned with their commitment to the team's values and in a neutral fashion, creates the space for us all to show up in new ways rather than perpetuating labels based on past patterns of behavior.

In order for Sharla to ask Curious Questions and engage in a Call Forward with Marvin, she needs to:

- Engage with herself and her frame of view first and consider where her point of view has originated

> "I am aware that Marvin's lateness activates my own survival pattern as a result of my own conditioning."

  □ This includes examining their own SuperLoop (what belief, biology, or behavior is causing them to fight, flight, disassociate, freeze, or appease).

- Acknowledge her own bias toward the given situation

> "I get that in my family being on time meant being fifteen minutes early. Marvin's conditioning was that as long as you weren't more than fifteen minutes late, it was acceptable. It's not about right or wrong; it's about doing what works for this current team."

  □ This includes examining how her own beliefs and history have influenced her perception of Marvin. Since Sharla came from a strict authoritarian household, she should examine her own bias toward that style of communication and personal presentation.

- Engage with this process with curiosity for Marvin—use Curious Questions to engage with Marvin's perspective

  - Sharla will ask questions that probe how Marvin arrived at particular conclusions and behaviors with a genuine intent for understanding him. This changes the situation to one of exploration rather than one that is conflict-oriented or trying to prove who is right or wrong.

> **"Marvin, I'm committed to creating a solution around this time pattern. Before we get to that, can you tell me about your expectations when you don't arrive on time?"**

When Sharla engages with Marvin using a Call Forward, one that makes use of Curious Questions, she might phrase it like this:

"I'm not sure if you are aware, but I've noticed that you've consistently been fifteen minutes late for our last few meetings. Is there something we can do to be more supportive in a way that will enable you to make the meetings on time?" This displays genuine curiosity and a need to understand what is going on for Marvin. Once we've established a real avenue of trust with this practice, we can be even more direct with our statements and be even more communicative: "I am frustrated, and I want to understand what is going on in your world."

Call Forwards offer data statements. The above account has a specific statement about the phenomena, namely when it's happened and how frequently. This is something Marvin can process and act upon. It provides context for everything else that will be said in the conversation. When your team crafts Call Forwards for each other, this is a critical step that ensures the conversation has clear boundaries and goals.

This Call Forward might continue with Sharla saying:

"I'm not sure if you are aware of the impact on the team, but we end up being late to our other meetings for the rest of the day. This can mean that we're off-schedule all week if we end up in a few meetings with you."

This further statement places the issue in the I/WE/ALL context. Marvin is now made aware of the pattern, has been given additional insight and support in elevating his performance, and is now aware of how the WE and ALL are affected by the pattern. Just as importantly, Sharla is now aware of Marvin's motivations, the context surrounding his actions, and of how she can support Marvin and lean into practicing Healthy Conflict to the benefit of the entire team.

This differs from the way that a conflict like this might go if the participants were ruled by amygdala hijack and instinct. If we don't design a way to engage in Healthy Conflict in our operations and practices, we will, inevitably, eventually engage in *unhealthy conflict* by default. The pressure builds up until it erupts, and then this conversation will be amygdala driven and the FFFDA model will come into play.

A version of this conversation driven by unhealthy conflict would be focused on the rhetoric of winning and domination rather than on problem-solving. Such language is usually laden with generalities and judgment: "You never listen to me. You don't care about this company. You're unprofessional."

Unhealthy conflict is filled with generalizations and attacks that activate the SuperLoop. It doesn't contain data statements or specifics, and it doesn't offer a way forward or a path to understanding. Unhealthy conflict is simply about satisfying the demands of the limbic system and securing one's sense of safety and satisfaction at the expense of the other party.

Calling Forward, Healthy Conflict, and Saying the Unsaid are critically important to organizations. Not Calling Forward sends the message that a given behavior is acceptable.

HUMAN VIBE: "SILENCE IS ACCEPTANCE." And this is especially true in teams, organizations, and groups. When it comes to organizational dynamics, saying nothing carries the significant risk of being translated by others as acceptance. If it is physically and psychologically safe, we should bring our ideas to others. We only have agency by making sure our voices are part of our organization's planning and consideration.

If we are accountable, when we have made a commitment and it is not kept, we need to communicate about it so that it does not seep into the culture.

The importance of this process is that it creates a space for a better, more collaborative working environment. This also creates psychological safety by giving us the ability to have more agency to discuss our working conditions and to learn from our peers. This is an opportunity for organizations to design the way to handle conflict rather than to just let the default occur.

The SuperLoop is always a factor in our behavior, and this presents a number of opportunities. Once someone is aware of their SuperLoop and their System 1 and 2 thinking, this awareness can act as a compass for the way our conditioning, biology, and socialization are affecting our perceptions and behavior. This is the very essence of Actionable Awareness.

Healthy Conflict engages with this compass and uses it to find a pathway that develops the I/WE/ALL and improves any aspect of an organization that is being impacted by our inability to handle stress, take response ability, and address its root causes.

The final goal of Calling Forward is to find a way forward that benefits everyone involved. This doesn't necessarily mean accommodating the desires of every participant—for Marvin, a win-win might be something like addressing his priority, adjusting his day-to-day schedule, or finding a different position or job that suits his needs and ability to engage with a certain workflow. Calling Forward also builds agency in Sharla, which, in turn, benefits the entire culture. Ultimately, this should be an outcome that benefits the I, WE, and ALL.

This Actionable Awareness, an awareness with solutions and commitments for future actions, was exactly what was needed in the culture of The Chopra Center.

The Chopra Center, SuperLoop, and Healthy Conflict

Ultimately, the challenges and opportunities The Chopra Center wanted to engage with were centered on the SuperLoop cycle and on Saying the Unsaid. That day in the conference room illustrated the way it influenced their decision-making, their teamwork, their relationship with leadership, and their perspective on the culture. On that day in San Diego, the team of The Chopra Center was being influenced in a number of ways. The core of that day that opened these two chapters was all about empowerment and building a high-functioning team. Those at the conference had studied the concepts of empowerment, Call Forwards, Peer-to-Peer Accountability, and Saying the Unsaid, and yet they had not acted upon these concepts because they had been overwhelmed by their own SuperLoop processes.

Our biology has been altered by the past experiences we've had when we spoke "out of turn." When we look into our past, how many of us could say that speaking up didn't agitate our parents? Aren't many people shunned for "causing trouble" when they pointed out things a family didn't want to hear? How many can identify with the fear of being seen as a "suck up" when we showed enthusiasm in our childhood classrooms? How many of us were the people who wanted to discuss money, politics, or religion at the dinner table?

We learned to avoid discussing what others did not want to hear from us. We learned to "go along to get along," and this impulse put us into a state of what SuperLoop Praxis calls Artificial Harmony. The people in that room on that day were practicing Artificial Harmony by not addressing the issue of their derailed meeting.

Many in the room were agitated and disappointed. The disconnect was clearly apparent and present—but not to Krista, who was in her own state of amygdala hijack from both the stress of the team's response to the election and then with the prospect of having disappointed her peer group.

Despite this clear sentiment in the room, everyone declined the opportunity to engage with that discomfort by trying to get their meeting back on track. Despite all the training everyone in that room had undergone, they were still not Saying the Unsaid. Rather, they had defaulted into the cultural, hierarchical norms that encouraged them to be seen and not heard—to engage in Artificial Harmony. Falling into these norms had consequences on several levels. For one, Krista was entirely unaware of their desires for the direction of the rest of the session. This meant that she, their leader, would be unaware of this pattern for the future—and thus that unhealthy, unproductive pattern might never be broken. Another consequence is that this behavior is in opposition to the values of a heart-centered organization, which is supposed to engage in egalitarian discussion and honesty. Defaulting to hierarchical Artificial Harmony made these values impossible.

Does this sound familiar? Do you often sit in meetings where an entire room refuses to say what they are clearly thinking? Isn't it frustrating that you know these issues will be discussed in text messages and around the proverbial water cooler after the meeting?

Why do we do this when it is contributing to the exact opposite of creating psychological safety and a healthy work culture, the team's needs, or the needs of the organization?

WHAT'S WORKING AND WHAT'S NOT WORKING (W4)

This is a structured process at G3 that involves an inventory of processes, results, and a meta-reflection on the I/WE/ALL. The strategies surrounding managing those processes come from multiple perspectives. This involves consistent, systematic reflection from individuals, teams, and leadership at regular intervals where these groups make it a day-to-day practice to consider the following: What's working? What was achieved? How was it achieved? What was the intention at the outset? What's not working? What was not achieved? Why was this not achieved? This process normalizes operational time for Saying the Unsaid and addressing the unaddressed so that teams can practice consistent Authentic Communication within their culture.

Do you or someone on your team have information that could get a person or the team's goals back on track, but instead of communicating it to the person or the group, they talk about it "around the water cooler" to everyone else? Please don't take it personally. I have seen this challenge with CEOs, midlevel managers and first-day employees. It is one of the biggest opportunities for transformation that awaits us all. However, *without creating the environment to practice these skills—starting with you—a business will continue to perpetuate dysfunctional environments. This extends outward from work to families politics, academia, and all the other global conversations that we all yearn to be part of to cocreate healing in our humanity.*

While this might seem like a conscious choice on the part of an individual or an organization, the behavior of engaging in conflict or avoidance is an extremely strong set of biological and psychological responses.

Most of us have been conditioned not to question, to accept top-down edicts, and to stay in line to avoid conflict and repercussions. We also are each handling our own direct experiences of the previous times we have stepped outside of these social norms and were punished for doing so. Because they were at least partially stuck in this flawed perception of leadership and accountability, the individuals at The Chopra Center hadn't intervened in that moment—despite the fact that they knew that the goal of the WE/ALL that day was to reflect upon their own agency and the results of a massive Equity Audit that had taken months to complete.

This difficulty happens in all organizations because every organization has some semblance of a traditional hierarchical leadership. People often sit back and wait to be ordered around by the leadership. They desire to avoid upsetting the order of things by simply not engaging in honest and open communication with their peers or their leaders. It's all too common for midlevel management to watch executives make mistakes consistently without intervening to support them while then complaining about the situation and leader later, out of earshot—all while not addressing the actual problem or supporting leaders in a way that they desperately need to be effective, fulfilled, and ultimately meet the needs of their teams and companies.

The key to progress for The Chopra Center was to change the culture's relationship to conflict. The employees there frequently avoided breaking the Artificial Harmony at work when something needed to be resolved. The Chopra Center, as a strong, heart-centered organization, needed to reorient their perspective so that it focused on the ALL, with the I and WE aspects of their culture focusing on carrying out that mission they had all agreed to undertake—one which starts with their accountability to themselves. They cannot carry out the commitments they have to each other without carrying out their commitments to themselves. Leadership is an inside-out job. Always.

Structures within an organization cause this as much as individual systems. This can include:

- Meeting formats that do not allow for a neutral meeting of ideas because they are designed by one person rather than allowing contributions from the WE/ALL

- Leadership that does not intentionally create space and time to give and receive input and FeedForward

- A culture that punishes deviations from cultural norms—even those that are constructive—by either social ostracizing or financial/hierarchical consequences

- A workflow that does not prioritize time for reflection and revision

Does *this* sound familiar? How often do you sit in a room where everyone knows something is wrong, but they displace that responsibility to another? Where people disempower themselves by choosing, by default or design, not to engage? In the fable "The Emperor's New Clothes," everyone laughed at the emperor for being naked even while missing out on one of the core meanings of the story—that the crowd around him is *enabling this lack of awareness*, making them as laughable as he was. Not a single person in the crowd had the courage to let him know that their entire country was being embarrassed. Only a child, a person with the least amount of conditioning or positional power, was willing to point out that the emperor was, in fact, naked. The swindlers and sycophants had too much to lose and were too used to not questioning the emperor, so, they left him, their country, and their event to fail despite knowing better.

As I worked to engage with these problems on that day in The Chopra Center conference room, I leaned in, trying for an even deeper level of Actionable Awareness, and asked the group in a slow, compassionate voice, "How often does this happen with the team? That you make a commitment, something or someone hijacks that priority, yet no one on the team leans in to redirect?"

I saw heads nodding and raised hands, and then someone said, "All the time."

"Ok, great," I told them. "Thank you all for your truth. Let's take ten minutes to identify the patterns of why this is happening and the team's commitment to behavioral changes moving forward—and let's use only a word or a short phrase to do it." I wanted to create structured boundaries for the process and to get some explicit buy-in from the room. "Is everyone aligned with what we're doing?"

I received a resounding "Yes!" from the room.

Then, I heard someone comment quietly to their teammate, "Good luck with that. We need an entire day just for this."

This was a comment I could have chosen to ignore. This person, however, was Saying the Unsaid—just not to his team.

So I modeled it for them, "Anyone hear what Miguel just said?"

In Humancentric Facilitation, an interruption (either directly or with a pause) that breaks Artificial Harmony for the sake of modeling Praxis is a critical skill. Knowing when to intervene or when to let something play out is absolutely critical. As my dear colleague Krista Petty, CEO and Founder of Boldly Embody Life, shares, "The Power of the Pause" is priceless. That day, I was modeling responsible leadership and behavior rather than engaging in Artificial Harmony so as not to upset Miguel or maybe the flow of the exercise.

A few heads nodded in agreement with most anyone else in earshot wondering if Miguel might be getting reprimanded for his seemingly sidebar comment.

"My request is for you all to trust the process and fully engage. Show of hands, can I count on y'all to do this?"

When we are transforming a new culture via Humancentric Facilitation, ignoring misaligned behaviors rather than using them to model transparency is one of the biggest mistakes we make. And we do it to protect our own discomfort. We get to model the fact that authentic transparency is messy and may be fraught with uncertainty. To complicate things, our biology translates that uncertainty as unsafe. I can't tell you how often breaking Artificial Harmony will also dump what feels like a gallon of adrenaline into my body at a moment where it isn't really warranted. As leaders, our ability to normalize the risk of practicing new behaviors is only as impactful as our ability to practice it consistently. Teams do what their leaders do, not what they say.

So I knew I had to model this properly. We had a timekeeper turn on the ten-minute alarm. We engaged in the process of popcorning (where one person starts the process, and when they are complete, they call out someone in the team to go next) for each person to say a word or phrase of why they thought the team did not intervene when the person leading their company-wide meeting went off track.

If someone went down the rabbit hole of more than a word or phrase, I interrupted them with, "Only a word or phrase." It was a new practice that needed the committed space and effort to become their new practice.

We were identifying patterns of behaviors explicit and implicit. By the third time I redirected someone, the whole room got it. Then, embracing their rediscovered agency, they began to redirect their peers!

We were interrupting each other for the greater good—even when it felt awkward or when they commiserated. We were so committed to this process that the interrupting, typically interpreted as rude, unprofessional, etc., was invited into the new behaviors. It was the true essence of Calling Forward. When there was clarity of purpose, it created new boundaries for all to succeed. It didn't feel offensive; it felt like unity.

The structure allowed freedom—the *Healthy Conflict* allowed freedom. We completed that task in ten minutes and aligned around recommitment to the practice of Saying the Unsaid. The feedback from the team was, "We should have done this months ago," to which another team member replied, "We did, in the training."

As leaders, we should understand that new training, specifically competency-based training, takes time and context to land in a way that is accessible for deeper application. As the widely used aphorism says, "When the student is ready, the teacher appears."

This created a sense of team responsibility and leadership that positively influenced the results of the next two days—but it also addressed larger patterns at The Chopra Center and their relationship with leadership.

LARGER PATTERNS

This might seem like a minor day in the history of The Chopra Center, but it was the beginning of conscious work to undo a much larger pattern that had taken root. The recommitment to Saying the Unsaid allowed them to change their relationship with their leadership in a way that helped them grow. They could be part of the problem or part of the solution—it was theirs to win or lose.

The issue that was at odds with their values and which was causing them organizational strife was the fact that they, against the values of the company, perceived their organization as a top-down hierarchy with Deepak Chopra at the top. They prized his skill, wisdom, and authority, so they left much Unsaid and instead waited on Deepak's leadership rather than acting on their own. They expected Deepak to provide authentic leadership, but this is structurally impossible without Peer-to-Peer Accountability, where they also hold themselves responsible for the culture of their organization.

Rather than taking responsibility for the problems in front of them, they waited on the leadership and grew resentful—just like that day in the conference room—which was only magnified by their inability to engage in Healthy Conflict. These individuals across the company needed to alter their perception so that they could regain their power and agency rather than waiting on someone else. They perpetuated the authoritative leadership model—one that was counter to their own values—and expected authentic results.

This created disharmony as they projected and blamed their leadership (in this case, Deepak Chopra) and consequently absolved themselves despite placing their leader in an impossible situation. How do we as leaders solve issues if our teams do not effectively communicate them?

HUMAN VIBE: "1 PROBLEM, 2 SOLUTIONS." If we identify an issue we also get to identify solutions. A leader ends up as the figurehead, and they can find themselves as the prime target for all criticism—regardless of whether that criticism is hypocritical.

The Chopra Center leadership was not hampered by these organizational issues because they were bad people or because of an ineffective work style. The problem was, in fact, quite the opposite. They actively fought against all the structures that perpetuate unhealthy conflict and stimulate amygdala hijack. They wanted to create an organization that eschewed toxic hierarchies and patriarchy, but they also lived in the legacy of those structures just by being set up as a vertically organized enterprise.

When a company reorients their perception of conflict to engage in Healthy Conflict, Call each other Forward, and Say the Unsaid, they emphasize and normalize the shared accountability each of us has within the culture we share. This shift in perception is only possible when we are able to reorient our engagement with the SuperLoop and manage our response to conflict. For The Chopra Center, this meant practicing the art of Healthy Conflict and Saying the Unsaid.

This leads to an individual agency that is based on the shared common goal rather than an organization that is based solely on following leadership passively (and then blaming said leadership for shortcomings within the company even though we did not take full repsonsibility to ensure we were communicating and creating action plans in alignment with leadership to create the results we all committed to). It also ensures Peer-to-Peer Accountability, which empowers all individuals to engage with each other when they see that an individual is off-mission and struggling. If we want an inclusive, authentic leadership model rather than a top-down authoritative model, then we all need to show up that way, not just the C-suite. It's often very easy to blame those in positions of power in the system rather than being Respond-Able to be the change we wish to see in the world.

Ultimately, The Chopra Center found their Actionable Awareness. They deemphasized the idea their leadership was solely responsible for the day-to-day culture-wide challenges they were encountering. Consequently, the culture of leaders being the sole focus of accountability began to shift as the individuals in the organization found their power and their ability to act. They were able to better utilize their values by no longer avoiding Healthy Conflict, by Calling each other Forward, and by Saying the Unsaid.

SAYING THE UNSAID

Making a sustained, directed practice of Saying the Unsaid normalizes authenticity and improves an organization's competencies in healthy conflict, communication, productivity, and its morale.

Saying the Unsaid creates three key outcomes:

1) Team members being responsible for contributing positive, negative, or unclear perspectives.

2) Team members are modeling communicating positive, negative or unclear perspectives

3) The organization is benefiting from the talent of all members by normalizing the practice of giving and receiving contrasting perspectives."

Within seven years, The Chopra Center was purchased by The Healing Company, and Deepak's primary focus became this evolution. The rapid increase in efficiency and value that attracted this purchase was in no small part a result of the cultural changes that the organization was able to facilitate by Operationalizing their Consciousness using SuperLoop Praxis.

Today The Chopra Foundation is still a leader in engaging with conscious business practices, operating at a scale and effectiveness that is surely enabled by their Actionable Awareness of the aspects of consciousness that most companies simply do not engage with. Deepak continues to lead the organization as its CSO (chief science officer).

Krista is now a SuperLoop facilitator and a CliftonStrengths certified coach with her own consulting practice. She was, and remains, a highly skilled practitioner in conscious business practices. Her efforts were absolutely critical to the growth of The Chopra Center and The Chopra Foundation. She currently guides hundreds of business leaders through engaging with SuperLoop Praxis and Gallup Strengths. Her courage to hear the Unsaid on that day and the awareness with which she engaged with her own SuperLoop remains a very inspiring moment in my career.

"Courage is the most important of all the virtues because without courage, you cannot practice any other virtue consistently."

—MAYA ANGELOU[35]

---

35 Maya Angelou, "Maya Angelou: Courage Is the MOST Important Virtue of All | Super Soul Sunday | OWN," *The Oprah Winfrey Show*, May 12, 2013, https://www.youtube.com/watch?v=o2HapMettMg.

"To thine own self be true, and it must follow, as the night the day, thou canst not then be false to any man."

—SHAKESPEARE, *HAMLET*, ACT I, SCENE III

CHAPTER FIVE

RESPONDABILITY

I n 2021, Massachusetts State Senator Diana DiZoglio ran for
the position of state auditor. This heated election became a
test of her ability to respond and ultimately made her one of
the most committed examples of conscious leadership I've ever
seen in my practice. In Massachusetts, the home of infamous political
dynasties like the Kennedys, politics is a full-contact sport—so it takes
fierce courage to be in the political arena.

Diana DiZoglio is the Massachusetts State Auditor who has
championed equality across her entire career. She is the youngest
elected Democratic woman in Massachusetts. She was born to a seventeen-year-old single mother who struggled with substance abuse,
and she grew up housing-and-food insecure while also being exposed
to domestic violence. Diana knew education would be her ticket to
a new life. When she graduated high school, she entered community
college, paying for it by waitressing, cleaning houses, and nannying.
She was then offered a scholarship to Wellesley College, a prestigious
institution known for its belief in the enduring importance of service

and putting that belief into practice. She became the first person in her family to have earned a college degree. She takes her responsibilities as an elected official incredibly seriously because, in her own words, she would not have had the life she has without the investment of the state and the taxpayers—and her chosen purpose is to ensure that those investments remain opportunities for the youth of our future.[36]

Diana is also a very dear friend.

We were connected by a mutual colleague in 2016 after Diana had defeated a local, very well-connected, state representative to make history by becoming the youngest female state representative at twenty-nine years of age. This mutual friend, in what would turn out to be a serious understatement, told me, "You have to meet her. You are going to love her."

At this point in her career, Diana was experiencing a paradox; on one end of the pendulum, she was having great success as a state representative, yet, on the other end, she was shining light on a chronic issue at the heart of antiquated systems—calling out inequities in state government. For her, the particularly controversial issue involved the use of nondisclosure agreements (NDAs) allowed for sexual harassment cases involving state government officials and their team members. Diana contended that the explicit use of these NDAs is to keep the victims quiet and that they serve no other reason that benefits the taxpayers or the function of the government. Ultimately, the only purpose of these NDAs is to protect the abuser and to keep the abused from telling their story if they seek justice.

Diana wrote, "These NDA documents are used very often by people in power to hide assault, to hide harassment.… They empower

36 Charles Duhigg, "What Google Learned from Its Quest to Build the Perfect Team," *New York Times*, February 25, 2016, https://www.nytimes.com/2016/02/28/magazine/what-google-learned-from-its-quest-to-build-the-perfect-team.html.

the perpetrator and allow them to move from victim to victim very easily."[37]

These cases were of particular importance to her because Diana had personally lived through a sexual harassment experience when she'd served as a legislative aide on Beacon Hill in 2011.

She was not supported by those in power during her sexual harassment case. In fact, she was told that she should "just get out of politics" by senior politicians. Diana is one of those humans who breaks down barriers. You tell her she can't, and she responds, "Watch me." This is especially true when that barrier is related to human rights or is inculcating an abuse of power.

Fast-forward ten years later to 2021. I reflect often about her decision to run for the office of state auditor, or as she coined it, chief accountability officer. During the COVID-19 pandemic, I found Diana in deep reflection. Was she really making a difference? How could she serve the constituents of Massachusetts where they were communicating to her that they needed it most? Diana is that leader who shares her cell phone number with all who ask. She spends much time engaging with the communities she serves. So she directly knew their pain points.

One of the chronic issues was government compliance. We had a deep conversation about her impact, her future, and how she could be in deeper service to the world. One day she declared, out of the blue, that she was thinking about running for state auditor. This was surprising. I wasn't even sure what an auditor did. Financial auditing? In fact, it is the position in charge of holding the government agencies and officials accountable for the contracts and budgets they receive.

---

37   "Diana DiZoglio Alleges Sexual Harassment at Massachusetts State House," CBS News, March 7, 2023, https://www.cbsnews.com/boston/news/ diana-dizoglio-sexual-harassment-state-house-massachusetts/.

She would run as chief accountability officer—leading the charge for transparency in state government to ensure tax payer dollars were executed according to the will of the people.

During the months leading up to the election, Diana came to my home, Serendipity Beach Retreat, and used it as a place to work, rejuvenate, and decompress while surrounded by nature. I was with her the day she received a call that required her to respond rather than react. I remember seeing her answer her phone and then bolt upright in shock and outrage.

Her campaign manager was calling to inform her that their political opponent in the state auditor's race had unearthed the fact that Diana had (as a teenager) worked as a youth counselor in a conservative evangelical church. Among its other radical beliefs, this religious organization did not accept the LGBTQIA+ community. Her opponent was now publishing this information in an effort to undermine DiZoglio's relationship with the LGBTQIA+ community, who were ardent supporters of Diana's campaign. Subsequently, her opponents ran tens of thousands of dollars in newspaper, television, and radio ads across markets far and wide. These ads tried to claim that Diana's time in these groups as a child and young adult reflected her current beliefs.

As we've discussed in previous sections, the human brain loves to track for certainty. We want to be able to categorize people easily. But people have the ability to change their beliefs. To grow and change past where they were as teenagers. Diana's beliefs had changed quite a bit as she'd grown up and left the church to find her own path. Her mother found refuge in this evangelical lifestyle, which is why Diana was there. Her mother's well-being was critical to Diana, even as a preteen. She was the proverbial child who parented her parent. She had to be responsible for her mother's sobriety, which included her mom's connection to this church.

Her opponent, however, had unearthed this aspect of her past and was now weaponizing it to end Diana's push toward creating an impact in the lives of her constituents across the state. The situation was clearly intense and overwhelming. The next call that came in was from the president of the largest LGBTQIA+ organization in the state. They were outraged at the audacity of the smear campaign, and even laughing at how ridiculous it was. This was Boston politics, though, and it was a serious situation—they wanted to discuss how they could support Diana in her next move.

Despite this, Diana chose to respond to these events rather than to simply react to them in kind. She let her values and her principles guide her actions. Diana had, in fact, also become aware of some negative behavior in her opponent. She'd discovered that he had a grim (and recent) history of domestic violence and contact with law enforcement. It was, to be certain, a dark side of his past life. His young daughter had even given testimony on record confirming the abuse. Despite this, and despite the urging of basically all of her senior advisors, Diana refused to air a counter-attack ad. To add fuel to the fire, her opponent was running on a platform of family values despite the fact that his personal history proved he had behaved ethically and morally against this campaign rhetoric.

Simply put, she didn't believe that elections should be run on issues that weren't policy related. She didn't want to undermine the process by resorting to mudslinging—she wanted to win on the basis of her commitment to the job and her policies. She knew that her performance was aligned with the LGBTQIA+ community, and that was what mattered. She had faith that they knew who she was and that she had acted as their representation in the government to the best of her ability. She was not going to play dirty politics.

Diana had a higher purpose, and she stuck with it no matter the outcome. She knew she was taking a big risk by not engaging in tit-for-tat politics, but her commitment to the sacredness of political work was more powerful than her fear of that risk.

On its face, this act might have looked like it was a decision based on morality or her values; she was personally against the idea of mudslinging. Maybe it was a decision made on behalf of her political party—she was committed to be part of the aspirational values rather than the typical establishment rules of mudslinging. Perhaps she valued the system too much to be someone who undermined it, and so she protected the very idea of electoral politics that is based on policy more than personality—a decision made on behalf of the ALL.

In reality, her decision wasn't driven by just one of these ideas; it was a response and not a reaction because it took into account *all* of these angles. Even more than this, she was able to respond, acting with Actionable Awareness, because she challenged her own perceptions, engaged with her own SuperLoop, and made certain that her choice was actually a choice. She engaged with her responsibilities, her beliefs, her history, and her biology.

If Diana had simply given in to her initial anger, hurt, or confusion and immediately crafted her own attack ad, she would have been reacting as an individual and not responding in a way that honored her values and goals. Diana had been immersed in SuperLoop and had become an avid practitioner after her training. SuperLoop Praxis was the foundation that gave her the space to consciously respond by design rather than defaulting to outside forces that wanted her to react.

As I've come to know and work with Diana, a major part of her political efforts have been to increase equity for those who have been the targets of harassment, discrimination, and abuse. She, even as a junior senator, actively sought to change laws in her state so that nondisclosure agreements could no longer be a part of settlement agreements reached by the state on issues of harassment, discrimination, and abuse.

Her belief, as a state senator, state auditor, and an individual, was that the use of nondisclosure agreements in such settlements was using state resources to silence the victims of sexual assault, discrimination, and harassment. This practice did not align with the fiduciary responsibility given to her by the oath of her position, as well as the constituents of the Commonwealth of Massachusetts.

Although this sounds like common sense, it ultimately became extremely controversial and served as a large source of tension for Diana as a politician. She quickly lost the support of many political colleagues who should have ostensibly been for a more transparent process. The top level of her party's leadership was so threatened by the proposed auditing of these previous settlements and the nondisclosure agreements associated with them that they formed a Super PAC that raised $500,000 and created media in an attempt to stop her from being elected to the Democratic seat as an auditor.

Nevertheless, Diana has persisted in this endeavor into 2024, continuing to push for both this new policy and the auditing of all governmental agencies led by powerful state figures.

Leaders are at their best when they are responding. In order to understand what this entails and why it's so critical, we must first explore the difference between a response and a reaction and how this concept is necessary for us to engage with our goals with true responsibility and accountability. Using this ability to respond and through engaging with the SuperLoop notion of RespondAbility, Diana was able to continually progress in her political career and bring her ethics and policies to the state level, expanding from a staff of 5 to a staff of over 230 people.

And, yes, Diana not only won the race for a Democratic party seat but also was elected as the youngest female auditor in Massachusetts history while establishing her place among the top five female leaders running the state—also a historical milestone.

Responsibility versus RespondAbility

"Between stimulus and response, there is a space. In that space is our power to choose our response. In our response lies our growth and our freedom."

—**VIKTOR E. FRANKL, *MAN'S SEARCH FOR MEANING*** [38]

You'll notice that the heading above bears a striking resemblance to the word "responsibility." This is no coincidence. RespondAbility ties directly into our elevated concept of how SuperLoop practitioners think of responsibility on the I/WE/ALL levels. This chapter will examine the notion of RespondAbility, how it's an evolution of our earlier practices surrounding perception and the SuperLoop, and how we stand to benefit from this rethinking of responsibility on every level of the I/WE/ALL.

Our typical notions of responsibility are goal oriented. "Will I deliver on my KPIs? Will I prioritize specific tasks? Will I meet annual goals?" This is indeed a core element of responsibility, but it falls short

---

38   Viktor E. Frankl, *Man's Search for Meaning*, translated by Ilse Lasch (Boston: Beacon Press, 2006).

of what is required for an individual to act in a conscious manner that will support the I/WE/ALL and allow it to thrive.

When we live in an unexamined, hierarchical mindset, we view responsibility as either a checklist or a personal means to an end. What we are responsible for is often a means of avoiding something unpleasant, achieving some material outcome, or making another person happy. It means carrying out a task or some other transactional experience because of the expectation of a reward or the avoidance of a punishment. In other words, these things are often obligations for the I, and they're usually based on hierarchy or duty.

Responsibility is rarely viewed in the context of the WE or ALL.

Inside of the G3 model, responsibility is not just about completing tasks that occur on the individual level; it is about maintaining the perception and awareness that will allow us to consciously "respond" to our lives rather than merely "reacting" to individual events and circumstances without considering their context, causes, and results (both external and internal).

Responding versus Reacting

The ability to be a conscious leader and to run a conscious organization ultimately involves the ability to differentiate between what constitutes a reaction and what constitutes a response.

Despite the seeming similarity of these terms, responding is very different than reacting. Responding constitutes a conscious, deliberate, proactive, thoughtful choice—it *is* practicing Actionable Awareness. Reacting, on the other hand, is involuntary. It's our mind and body taking a knee-jerk action due to some outside stimuli. We don't truly have control of the process of reacting any more than we have control over our reflexes.

Which makes responding incredibly important for those who are operating conscious organizations. They have responsibility for the I/WE/ALL levels of their organization and do not have the luxury of reacting on reflex. G3 has created the concept of "RespondAbility," an ontological tool that enables us to examine our perceptions, our biology, and our history to ensure that we are reacting to the conditions and values in front of us rather than reacting to other factors that are not as immediate or material as they might seem in the moment.

Engaging in RepsondAbility involves utilizing the G3 understanding of both perception and the practice of Actionable Awareness of one's SuperLoop. We must acknowledge that our perceptions of a given situation are incomplete because they are conditioned by our past experiences, the environment, and our biology. These factors will always be part of the GPS our brains try to use to navigate the opportunities and challenges we encounter, and our ability to interpret those signals is critical to the success of the I, WE, and ALL.

Let's consider a scenario that illustrates these principles, starting with a person who is a reactive type:

REACTING AS A DEFAULT RESPONSE

Reactive individuals will engage with scenarios without considering their limited perceptions in their SuperLoop. Gregory is an individual who many of his colleagues describe as a "hot reactor," an individual who is prone to reacting out of anger, anxiety, and with his immediate gut instinct. When Gregory runs into adversity, he barrels through it, grabbing on to his initial perception of a situation as the absolute truth. When Gregory finds someone who disagrees with him, he will often vehemently argue for his point of view.

In our hypothetical, Gregory is someone who has built up a reputation as an aggressive go-getter. He's quick to react to a change in circumstances. He's especially known for reacting hotly to any perceived threats to his leadership or his organization. The entire office knows that you don't step on Gregory's toes. Gregory calls out anything he sees as a mistake, and he does so publicly. Gregory is also charismatic, passionate about his desire to make a difference, and often the life of the party. This combination of charm and perceived competence initially draws others in to engage with him. His inevitable tendency to be a reactive person, however, often has team members, friends, and family keeping their distance so as not to have to walk on eggshells around him.

This has resulted in some impressive client acquisitions because, at first, people like Gregory's take-no-prisoners attitude, but it's also inevitably resulted in inadvertently siloing others because people are sometimes hesitant to approach him. Unbeknownst to Gregory, people don't want to be exposed to the likelihood of publicly being criticized, so they avoid him when there is a possibility of getting a negative reaction from him.

Despite his efficiency at acquiring new clients and his capability at leading those who work well in high-pressure environments, Gregory doesn't notice when client onboarding has begun to suffer due to a lack of communication with the WE. Gregory's tendency is to *react* to stress rather than to respond to it with Actionable Awareness. This behavior inevitably has begun to hurt the WE by creating an environment where his team communicates less and less with him, and consequently, they have less to contribute to the ALL. Gregory's tendency to yell, get angry, and otherwise react aggressively to stress has impacted his ability to deliver the strategic results he was hired to achieve—and all of this has happened in spite of his abilities and charisma.

Organizations enable this behavior when they do not prioritize the skill of practicing RespondAbility. An organization that doesn't address this issue also perpetuates the "blame-shame game," where the leader blames the lack of effectiveness on their team and the team blames their lack of effectiveness and Authentic Communication skills on the leader.

Both result in neither the team nor its leadership holding themselves accountable for their behaviors while all are actively engaged in creating an unsafe psychological work environment by undercutting many of the categories that can make work safe.

RESPONDABILITY (RESPONSEABILITY)

In a very similar parallel universe, there exists another Gregory who is almost the same as our first Gregory. This Gregory has trained in conscious inside-out work. This Gregory is cognizant of the aspects of his being that enable him to respond with Actionable Awareness. He knows his own SuperLoop. He is aware he tends to think of threats first rather than opportunities, and he knows that his knee-jerk reaction tends to be to imagine the motives of others to be self-serving and counter to his own. He, biologically, tends to react with a "fight" reflex when he's confronted with the kind of stress that activates his amygdala. His childhood with a whole gaggle of brothers and a strict father shaped him this way. He's also aware that his behavior, when he doesn't regulate it, can come across as threatening or domineering even when he doesn't intend it.

That's the environment he was raised in, and he's comfortable in such an environment—it was, after all, what he knew—and that environment even caused him to learn how to be charismatic and personable. The other survival behaviors imprinted on his SuperLoop, however, no longer serve him, so he has learned new skills. He is aware of how some people will have their SuperLoops activated by interacting with people like him, so he practices regulating his behavior with an increased sensitivity to the reactions of those around him. He still uses his ability to command a room, but he's now conscious enough to use it when it's most effective and to show consideration when he's deploying this style. He is consciously leading with his strengths and skills rather than being unconsciously led by default.

I, personally, can relate to Gregory—not in the sense that I'm aggressive, but because I'm very excitable and high-energy. I can be very effusive, productive, and multifocal. I tend to dive into projects completely and to immediately produce a large amount of work, references, and leads for the future. I get more energy from the possibilities that are being presented, and I love the exhilarating creative power I can feel as a project begins to gain momentum and manifests as a tangible reality in the world.

Through my years of practice at these concepts, I've become highly attuned to the fact that I get to practice RespondAbility in the way that I manage my energy, my communication, and my workflow. I've come to learn, from considering the perspective of others and the varying work styles of my peers, that this style doesn't work for everyone else no matter how well it fits my biology and my history. This default way I have of being was very definitively shaped by being in a huge, excitable family that loves to get loud.

I've seen that my effusive responses are daunting to some of my peers. They are overwhelmed by the amount of information I'm giving them, so I need to parse out my responses to them and to take some time to consolidate my thoughts so that they're conveyed in one message rather than being spread across several messages and calls. It is a practice of refining my adaptive coping mechanisms created over many years to ensure it includes the needs of those around me (the WE) and the goals we are committed to (the ALL).

I know that both leadership and good work are not just about me expressing myself (which very often it is acting out from past conditioning) at the expense of the needs of those around me. It is about practicing inclusion and belonging in a way that makes it safe for others to be themselves as well.

Operationalizing RespondAbility

The tools surrounding RespondAbility have research underpinning their efficacy. In 2012, Google launched an internal program, Project Aristotle, that explored why some teams succeed more easily than others. The name of the project is a reference to Aristotle's famous truism, "The whole is greater than the sum of its parts."

Google's researchers examined a wide variety of factors at work in their teams; this included how the teams were organized, the personalities and traits of the team members, the type of work they did, and the management styles overseeing their teams.

Interestingly, and unexpectedly to many, Google's researchers found that many factors that most would consider as core contributors to the effectiveness of a team mattered less than expected when it came to a team's efficacy. Practical wisdom would indicate that team members' interactions, the management styles, and the individual skills of coworkers would be the determining factors, but these were not the elements that indicated whether a team would be successful. Instead, the following factors were identified as being the foremost predictors of team effectiveness:

- **Psychological safety**—Team members feel comfortable taking risks and being vulnerable.

- **Dependability**—The team is composed of people who reliably complete quality work on time.

- **Structure and clarity**—Everyone has a clear role, plans, and goals. Everyone understands what is expected of them, and the path to meeting that expectation is clear.

- **Meaning**—The work has significance, which can be communicated and measured.

- **Impact**—Work is purposeful and makes a material difference in the world. Because Operationalizing Consciousness is all about creating value and Operationalizing it, the practice necessitates having a practical impact on both the organization and the world.

The findings of Project Aristotle were surprising to Google, but they highlighted foundational elements that must be at work if a company wants to be response minded instead of merely reactionary. The work from Project Aristotle radiated outward, inspiring a number of seminal works of business literature, including one of my personal favorites, *Search Inside Yourself: The Unexpected Path to Achieving Success, Happiness (and World Peace)*, by Chade-Meng Tan, a book about the incredibly important role of mindfulness in leadership.

The project demonstrates that providing consistent practices to intentionally develop these behaviors into the work environment of your organization increases the likelihood that your peers will be responding more often than they are reacting. Creating an environment of psychological safety within your organization increases the likelihood that employees will be transparent and open with their peers, making the space for a genuine response even in the face of difficult scenarios. Dependability as a cultural trait creates trust. "I can count on you to make and keep your commitments" is what functioning teams are built on.

This is true of organization-wide clarity as well, not just on the peer-to-peer level. When an organization has structure and clarity, it creates buy-in and the ability of the team to maximize performance because they can focus on the results rather than other factors. Clearly communicated beliefs about the purpose of our work enable individuals and teams to respond to events in the context of the organization's core values. The vision and mission become the north star to our behaviors and how we show up as a team.

Finally, when an organization is able to clearly measure and demonstrate how it has an impact on the world (and how this is done in a meaningful fashion), it enables those within it to collectively respond with that impact in mind rather than from their single limited perspective.[39]

TOOLS FOR USING RESPONDABILITY

A conscious individual views their ability to respond as a means of enacting agency—and a conscious company creates an environment that encourages the practice of that ability. We have the ability to respond rather than react, and thus we have the ability to impact our lives as conscious individuals. Intentionally tapping into the SuperLoop and using Actionable Awareness to develop the skill to respond rather than react means we are using our emotions and biology rather than those systems using us.

---

39   Bea Poyton, "Google's Project Aristotle," *Psychological Safety*, March 28, 2024, https://psychsafety.co.uk/googles-project-aristotle/.

When we are unconscious of our SuperLoop, we are not aware of our beliefs and perceptions. In this state, we give our power and agency to all the seemingly outside forces—"I've been like this my whole life, it's in my DNA, it's because I'm a Taurus, it's because I'm Italian, I'm a man and men have needs, it's sister stuff, I'm the leader, and (one of my favorites) it's just business," or any of the other myriad justifications we use when we are looking for a reason to excuse our behavior.

And yes, of course, all these circumstances may be true for you as well. They influence you, but they do not determine you, unless you let them. Accessing your SuperLoop to work for you rather than against you gives you your power back. It creates agency in its highest form. You get to be RespondAble for all your results, all the ways you want to be in the world, as a leader, a partner, a parent, a sister or brother, a friend, a mentor, rather than the world imposing on you from your past conditioning and societal expectations. In this model of behavior, responsibility isn't about culpability or obligation—responsibility means creating tangible results. A conscious individual is not responsible merely because of outside forces but rather because they are taking on the quest to enact the forces they want at work in the world and to elevate themselves to their best incarnation.

A major part of this practice is the recognition that much of what seems external—and thus beyond our ability to influence—is actually internal.

Which means it's in our control.

HUMAN VIBE: "IF IT'S TO BE, IT'S UP TO ME."
This Human Vibe recognizes that we cannot expect the results we want to appear to come from anyone but ourselves. This doesn't mean that we should act as lone wolves or eschew teamwork, but rather that we get to first lead with new behaviors and surround ourselves with those who expect the same from themselves.

Often, when we shirk responsibility for a given situation, we are externalizing something that is really internal—making the solution to a problem external ("I can't do my job if Jimmy won't do his") is giving away one's power. If the problem is "out there," then I have no power and become the victim. If I enact agency and bring solutions in both mindset and behaviors, then I am now part of the solution, even though the problem may not be fully solved.

It's worth mentioning that some problems can't be as easily influenced by people who are subject to others in a power structure—I am well aware that not every problem is within our control, but the act of at least seeking a solution *is*. If enough of us within an organization believe there are external solutions to our problems, we begin to affect the health of our entire organization. A conscious individual looks for solutions within themselves when they are faced with a challenge. We cannot force anything outside of us to act, change, or shift unless we do so with our own actions first. Too often, we project that the solution to our problem is "out there" and absolve ourselves of needing to act on our own.

Part of not externalizing our problems is recognizing how much our perceptions create these problems. Many of our day-to-day problems are actually internalized past experiences that we have turned into beliefs and rules and applied to the present. Engaging with responsibility is engaging with this awareness in an actionable manner and dealing with the facts of the current context rather than our projections upon it.

This means finding the origin of our beliefs and feelings and then exploring those origins so that we don't base our current actions on what we've experienced in the past. "Is my boss, Kenisha, aggressive, or am I working off the experience I had with my overly aggressive first boss and consequently unusually sensitive to Kenisha as a result of my past conditioning? Is my boisterous behavior positive and professional, or am I used to my loud family who likes to argue? Although I'm trying to add lightheartedness to meetings, am I unaware of the ways that I am distracting others and diverting our team focus by monopolizing the communication?"

One way to gauge this is to ask yourself and then a trusted friend, "Is my response commensurate with the situation, or do I seem as if I am being hypersensitive compared to how others might translate this situation?"

One of my experiences with a team member illustrates this set of practices and possibilities perfectly. Katie was a fabulous leader on one of my education teams. She came to work with us as a coach and curriculum specialist. She was extremely high performing, consistently earning accolades from her coworkers and exceeding the results that were expected of her. She had a high level of competence and character. Everyone loved working with her because of her deep respect for her team members and because of the years of knowledge she put to work in supporting and developing skills in others.

Katie reported to Marguerite, whose style of communication was very different from Katie's. Marguerite had a high level of competence, but she was also very direct and somewhat distant. She'd graduated from an Ivy League school and was an accomplished academic. Her character abilities and her emotional intelligence were still emerging during her leadership. She was not always naturally aware of how her behavior impacted others. Katie valued Marguerite's intelligence, but they had also come to experience tension on a number of levels. Katie was increasingly finding it difficult to work with Marguerite because of her terse and perfunctory disposition. Katie finally requested a meeting with me to discuss some deep concerns she had about her working relationship with Marguerite. As this came to a head, we scheduled a Connection Time session so that I could provide mentorship and an opportunity for reflection.

Katie was disturbed by her perception of Marguerite's professional affect. She shared how absolutely out of line she believed Marguerite's leadership style was and that it, in fact, did not reflect our mission or core values. She recounted her experiences working with Marguerite and relayed that others on the team had experienced similar interactions. She added that, based on our strong values and the fact that "most people" knew how challenging Marguerite was to work with, these issues with Marguerite needed to be addressed by the CEO.

Katie, being such a methodical person, had been thinking about this for several months before she approached me. This conflict was impacting her ability to such an extent that she was thinking of leaving the company altogether despite the success she was achieving and her love for her position. So we processed how these behaviors were impacting the results and psychological safety of the team.

Because Human Vibes are the shorthand we use to engage with complex concepts at G3, Katie asked me a question—What Human Vibes did I think best applied to this situation? I, curious as to her point of view on this matter within our culture, actually asked her if she'd mind telling me which Vibes she thought best applied to this situation:

Katie proceeded to share two Human Vibes she believed were applicable here: "silence is acceptance" and "no accountability, no credibility." She said she wanted to ensure she was not silently accepting this behavior and that if we didn't hold Marguerite accountable, we would lose credibility.

I acknowledged her proactive thinking and the fact that she'd considered these problems through the lens of her organization. Wanting to examine the issue from another perspective, I asked her if others on the team were as emotionally activated by Marguerite's behavior as Katie was.

She paused and commented, "Well, they absolutely do not like it and are afraid to address it with her for fear of retaliation." Sensing that this might relate to Katie's personal perceptions, I reiterated my question—I wanted to know if the rest of her team was as activated by this situation as she was.

She, sighing, clearly wasn't eager to engage with this but admitted that she was more affected by Marguerite's demeanor than the others. One of the Human Vibes is "I am never upset for the reason I think I am." I asked Katie to engage with this Human Vibe for a week and then to come back to me for another meeting.

Two days later, Katie approached my door and asked if I had another fifteen minutes. She entered the office, closed the door behind her, sat down, and then began crying.

"Susan, I'm so sorry for being so upset, but I think I'm realizing what it is."

She shared how when she identified her feelings—frustrated, oppressed, marginalized, protective—and thought about when she had felt this way before, she had a huge breakthrough.

"I went to Catholic schools, and my third-grade teacher, Sr. Jermaine, was demeaning, harsh, and verbally abusive to my classmates and me. Our parents trusted the school, so even though we complained back in those days, the adults were not to be challenged. When I am around Marguerite, that's how I feel—like I am in third grade and cannot do anything to impact this behavior. I feel victimized for myself and the entire team, but it's about my past and my SuperLoop as much as the actual experience in front of me."

Together we created a plan for addressing this with Marguerite using the Clearing Conversation process described below. I offered to support them by being part of the conversation. She asked for additional coaching, then replied that she felt confident enough to address it, thanked me, and said she would follow back up.

This process did not immediately solve the entirety of Marguerite's conflicts with Katie, but it was the first step. Marquerite, after the Clearing Conversation, continued to work on this conflict and even directly asked for coaching toward a more approachable leadership style.

Most importantly, what this process did was empower Katie to create agency for everyone involved by giving them a chance to address the conflict rather than be carried along by its momentum. They were given the opportunity to be RespondAble and to own how our experiences and environment are the architects of our mindbody.

Katie and Marguerite continued to work together for many years, creating great impact for the entire organization. To this day, Katie points to that shift in her perception as a moment that changed her life, her relationships, and her leadership from victim to empowered.

SuperLoop Praxis has several tools that are intended to develop our RespondAbility rather than reacting. These tools also allow for a deeper examination of the I/WE/ALL inside of an organization. The first of these tools is a variation on what I described above, a means of clearing tension from an organization.

HUMAN VIBE: "TOILET PAPER ON THE FOOT."

This Human Vibe describes the necessity for honesty about the things we observe. Everyone is familiar with the fact that they would want to know if they had a glaringly obvious issue (like toilet paper stuck to their heel as they left the restroom), even if it's embarrassing in the immediate moment. That sort of consistent honesty is the only kind of honesty that enables change. It creates an environment of safety, as you know your teammates "have your back." It also facilitates Peer-to-Peer Accountability rather than an authoritative model where it is the supervisor's responsibility to address team performance concerns rather than empowering agency for the entire system.

Steps of Clearing Conversations

Clearing Conversations, like the conversation I engaged in with Katie above, are critical tools in engaging with tension or conflict within an organization. This section lays out the steps of a Clearing Conversation and potential prompts to engage with these steps.

1. Acknowledge the relationship you have to the person you are communicating with and their value to you.

2. Share the patterns you noticed in yourself and are clearing. This shows that you're aware that all interactions have two sides and that you are aware of your responsibility (and RespondAbility) related to the circumstances you are discussing.

3. Take responsibility for your own pattern that got in the way. This enables everyone in the exchange to see that you are committed to working on these items in the future and are aware of them in the current moment. This, in turn, encourages responsibility in both parties involved in the Clearing Conversation.

4. Take responsibility. Make a direct statement about the issue and impact you want to address. For instance, "I am noticing that work has been unevenly assigned and completed by our team and that you are doing a majority of the work."

A Few Additional Prompts:

- "The stories I made up about *you* prior to engaging in this conversation are …"

   This prompt further acknowledges the varying perceptions that are possible of the same events. It specifically addresses that an individual can have a flawed understanding of the actions and motivation of their peers.

- "The stories I made up about *myself* prior to this conversation are …"

   This prompt allows the speaker to examine their perceptions of themselves and their motivations in a given situation.

- State how you have contributed to the issue or challenge. As an example, "I was wrapped up in my own responsibilities and didn't say anything when I noticed the issue."

- Invite the other person to share their perspectives. For example, "I sense the majority of the work has been completed by you and I am interested in understanding how this landed for you." When X happened, this is how I experienced it. This was the impact, intentional or not.

This acknowledges both the perspective of the speaker and the perspective of the recipient.

5. Request perspective that enables a productive conclusion for the Clearing Conversation and contributes to future Authentic Communication.

   □ Can you share with me how my communication is being received during this process?

   □ Generously listen to what the other person is communicating in both words and behaviors.

   □ Restate what you have listened to in both words and behaviors.

   □ Is there anything I could have done to make this process more effective?

6. Create a win-win agreement.

   □ Each party should communicate their desire outcomes for this conversation: "My request is …"

   □ Agree on a committed action(s) to create desired results and/or solutions.

   □ Acknowledge the commitment of both parties to the new behaviors: "What you can count on from me is …"

      » "My commitment moving forward is …"

Here are a few additional prompts we can use to exercise Respond-Ability during Clearing Conversations:

1. Ask permission: "May I clear with you?"

   It is important to ask permission to ensure both parties are open to it rather than either feeling blindsided or hijacked. Clearing can be an intense, focus-oriented process that requires time, concentration, and a conscious mindset. Not every moment is appropriate to conduct a Clearing Conversation any more than every moment is a good moment for a performance check-in.

2. Declare your intention: "My intention is to create clarity, to clear what I'm perceiving as Unsaid, and to align regarding how we can work together in a way that meets both our needs."

   This statement is articulating what you want for the relationship rather than focusing on what you don't want. This ensures that your motives and desired outcomes will be transparent and approachable.

3. Clear your fear: "I am nervous/anxious/worried/excited that what I say might ..." Conclude with a definitive, transparent statement, like "... impact you negatively/feel hard/harsh or may interfere with our relationship moving forward."

   This explicitly creates vulnerability that starts the conversation with you modeling openness. It recognizes aspects that have blocked this conversation from happening in the past. It also level sets any power dynamic that might get in the way. This invites the participants to give themselves a greater opportunity to respond rather than going with their initial reactions.

RespondAbility, of course, is not all about conflict. It's also about sharing perspectives and further exploring our own perspectives. To that end, affinity groups and employee resource groups can be amazingly effective aids to engaging with RespondAbility.

FINDING RESPONDABILITY WITH OUR PEERS

Peer affinity groups are places where groups with common identities and aspirations can regularly meet to discuss issues that are unique to their experiences or underrepresented in their wider organizational culture. The purpose of these groups is threefold: the first is to provide a place to create solutions to the problems that system impacted groups face inside of structures that were built by individuals with more hegemonic origins. The second is to leverage the unique perspective those in the affinity groups can utilize to create strategies, partnerships, and mutual support that wouldn't necessarily occur in more Eurocentric, patriarchal, or heteronormative environments. The third is to integrate the practices of Peer-to-Peer Accountability, the foundation of an authentic leadership culture.

There are many types of innovation that are blocked by traditional notions of identity, leadership, etc. Our worldviews are all different, and affinity groups are safe spaces that offer mentorship, provide an ability to engage in problem-solving and Peer-to-Peer Accountability, help us create supportive social networks, and improve employee retention. A study published in *Harvard Business Review* demonstrated that where traditional diversity programs fail to yield good results for the organization, affinity groups found success.[40]

In the SuperLoop framework, peer affinity groups are structured to be effective and conscious. They are meant to encourage responding over reacting, engaging with the goals of the I/WE/ALL as people consider their identities, interests, and the relationship these facets of their lives have to their work. These affinity groups feature a leader who is trained to provide facilitation and structure. Differing individuals within affinities will have different needs from a group, and a professional trained to lead such groups is a priority to ensure the group is effective for everyone involved.

An affinity group for young professionals might yield a career-long network. A group for LGBTQIA+ employees can ensure that policies and practices don't overlook gender and orientation. A group based around race and ethnicity can make sure that everyone's interests and cultures are considered as part of the ALL. A group committed to implementing SuperLoop will create an effective culture committed to maximizing the highest potential and performance. Affinity groups are an important structure to create a place for Saying the Unsaid to become a catalyst for advocacy, awareness, and positive change. Affinity groups are a place to practice new competencies such as responding versus reacting. A peer affinity group can provide a greater sense of context, history, and alignment that gives deeper insight to both our perception and the perceptions of our peers while intentionally creating a place to practice new skills.

Peer affinity groups in a conscious company are solution-oriented, using the "one problem, two solutions" model. They actively pursue

---

40   Frank Dobbin and Alexandra Kalev, "Why Diversity Programs Fail," *Harvard Business Review* 94, no. 7 (2016), https://scholar.harvard.edu/dobbin/publications/why-diversity-programs-fail.

solutions for the issues they identify from relating their common experiences. That makes these groups powerful platforms for strengthening and growing an organization and bringing their collective voices to the table.

Encoding and Decoding—What Seems Clear Isn't Always Clear

ENCODING AND DECODING

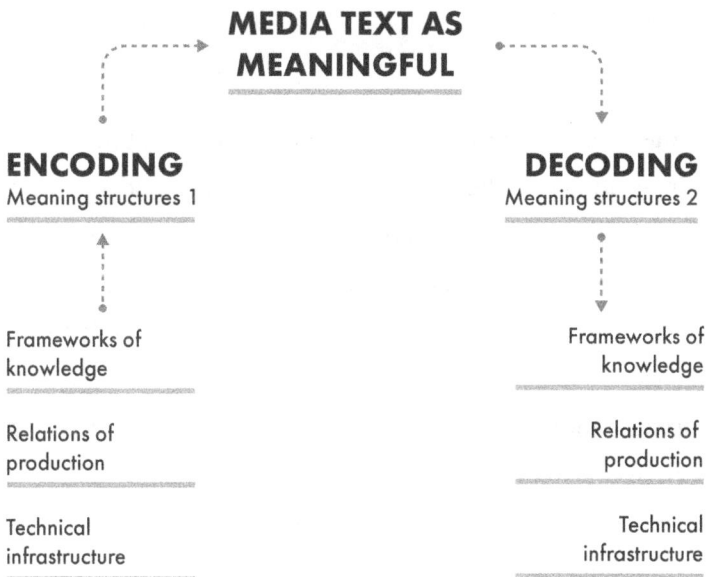

MEDIA TEXT AS MEANINGFUL

ENCODING
Meaning structures 1

DECODING
Meaning structures 2

Frameworks of knowledge

Relations of production

Technical infrastructure

Frameworks of knowledge

Relations of production

Technical infrastructure

Source: Encoding and decoding model (Hall, 1973).

HUMAN VIBE: "WE JUDGE OTHERS BASED ON BEHAVIOR, YET WE JUDGE OURSELVES BASED ON INTENTION." One idea that works particularly well in being able to respond rather than to react is to think about communication as a process of "encoding" and "decoding." This terminology originates from the media theorist Stuart Hall. He wrote about the fact that our communication occurs in three stages that complicate the way we interpret it. Communicating isn't as simple as we tend to think it is. We usually think that we conceive of an idea, say it, and that this idea will be transmitted, intact, to the person we are trying to communicate with.[41]

Hall noted that we start with an intended message, but that we then dress it up for both the purpose of the message and for the way in which we are attempting to communicate. In the media, this might be a song or a commercial, but when we are communicating in person, we might think of how differently we communicate, taking the others' interaction style into consideration. Businesses and organizations also use varying types of media—consider how different your communication can be on a phone call, an email, or a text message. Ultimately the message we intend to send is shaped by *how* we send it. It's encoded into the media we use and the language we use, and our original intention has now been shaped into something different. What would be a friendly chat in person necessarily becomes terser and more business-like via text. Your tone of voice gives a lot of information that an email simply can't.

---

41   Brian L. Ott and Robert L. Mack, *Critical Media Studies: An Introduction*, 3rd ed. (Hoboken: Wiley-Blackwell, 2020).

Much of this might be something you've ruminated on before, but we need to take the idea further. We start with information we want to communicate. Our ideas are, as Hall describes, then encoded into the way we choose to communicate them. They're altered again when we send them. What people don't often consider as closely is the fact that the receiver of these ideas must now "decode" what they've been sent. They will view this idea through their own social framework, their personal history, and their biology.

A well-known series of case studies used by Hall describes how in the movie *Die Hard*, there is a scene where terrorists blow up a number of police cruisers during the siege of an office building. Most viewers see this as a scene of tension. Things are being destroyed; people might be hurt. Hall, who was studying media reception in different contexts, was observing a viewing of *Die Hard* in a homeless shelter and was shocked to see that this audience was cheering throughout this scene. This audience, who had mostly had negative encounters with the authority figures, viewed this scene in a way that was not only different than how most viewers would receive it, but was actually the opposite of how the makers of the film intended for the scene to be viewed at all.[42]

Over the years, Hall studied many audiences, polling their reactions to various types of media, making note of the fact that different symbols and messages decoded differently for different audiences.

The importance of Hall's ideas for a business setting lies in focusing on the "encoding and decoding" element. If we're aware of this process, we can think more carefully about how information is sent and received. We can also train ourselves to be aware of how our own decoding of information and media is shaped by our beliefs, biology, and histories.

---

42   Ibid.

Hall found that the reactions of audiences could fall into three categories:

- **Accepting**: They encoded and received the intended message of a piece of media as expected by the person sending the message.

- **Rejecting**: The person has decoded the message and has largely arrived at a rejecting stance toward their conclusion about the intention of the message. Note that they do not necessarily accept or reject the original message, but that they instead are dealing with their perception of the message.

- **Negotiating**: The individual receiving the message has determined what they do and do not accept from the piece of media. They do not wholly reject or wholly accept the ideas being introduced to them. This decision has been influenced by their decoding and understanding of the message.

The most important information we can take away from these ideas is that potential variation of what can be received from the same message is broad. We all think we take different points of view in mind, but we rarely think about just how wide that range can be and at how many points it can be interpreted. As Ellen Galinsky said, "we must think about what we are trying to say and how we are going to say it if we want to communicate effectively and with intention." Equally important, we must think about how we receive information. What is someone trying to say, and how are they trying to say it?[43]

This framework for understanding communication may seem daunting. It's far less certain than the way we usually think of passing

---

43   Ellen Galinsky, *The Breakthrough Years: A New Scientific Framework for Raising Thriving Teens* (New York: Flatiron Books, 2024), Kindle edition.

ideas, which previous chapters in this book identified as the "injection model," the premise that your idea leaps, unchanged, from your head to the mind of another when you are attempting to communicate.

Thinking of our communication in this new framework reveals why it is so critical that we make a practice out of responding rather than reacting. As we've learned, after all, we have many factors influencing our gut reactions to what's in front of us—we need to navigate our perceptions and beliefs—our SuperLoop—as part of our efforts to work in a conscious manner and create an organization that is capable of practicing its values. It is a committed practice; it doesn't just happen merely because we intellectually know the framework.

HUMAN VIBE: "TO KNOW AND NOT TO DO IS NOT TO KNOW." Like many of the forces in this book, simply neglecting our penchant for reactionary behavior will leave these patterns to play out free of any checks or balances—most of the conflict, politicking, and complaining we see in the workplace is a result of a lack of communication, miscommunication, or a flawed reception of communicated data.

Balancing Our Responses and Finding Our Power

Part of our responses involves choosing how to temper our individual needs, the needs of our team, and the needs of the ALL. Self-expression is a critical component of well-being. The more we're doing work that we care about, the more we will be personally invested and the more we tend to be emotionally attached to the work we do. That attachment can be a huge asset and means of driving our work. Someone, for instance, who cares deeply about protecting someone's hard-earned property would make an excellent insurance agent. They'll empathize with their clients and want to get them the best outcome because they, on an emotional level, understand how important their work is.

On the other hand, that attachment and emotion can also get in the way of our professionalism, our perceptions, and the outcomes we want from our work. If that same insurance agent became too emotionally invested in a given situation, they might not be able to effectively gather information, process claims for damages, or deny a claim when it isn't relevant to the policy. Their empathy might overwhelm their responsibility to the WE/ALL levels of their organization and lead them to manage their emotions without considering their responses.

HUMAN VIBE: "EMOTIONS ARE A PERSONAL RESPONSIBILITY." This vibe has been referenced in previous chapters, but it takes on a new import when we consider all the elements we've learned about thus far—our ability to respond, our SuperLoop, and our perceptions are all critical factors in how we process our emotions. Emotions can be part of a healthy, helpful response, or they can be part of a negative response that hinders. Once we've learned these conscious tools, we can see emotions not as something that must be expressed immediately and outside of our control but instead as something we can manage and even use as the healthy tool for measuring our internal reality. *We handle* *our emotions, or they handle us.*

Self-regulation is a competency of executive function (the skills for regulating behavior, directing focus, and achieving defined outcomes), as well as a strength and an opportunity. When we are aware of the origin of our emotions and how we respond to them, we get to have more influence on ourselves and our environment. This gives us the ability to embrace that the majority of what we feel is external to us is actually internal. As Daniel Kahneman's Nobel Peace Prize–winning work detailed, *projection proceeds perception*; our history, biology, and beliefs are the things that tell us how to process and perceive the world. Once we own this, our understanding that more of our responses are in our control than we first believed, we have a greater ability to honor our responsibilities to ourselves, our team, and our missions and goals. If something is truly external to us, it limits our control. It has us. Understanding that much of our navigation of the world is internal allows us to claim power over the things that we believed had power over us.

When we allow something to dictate how we react to it, we are giving up our power. When we determine how we respond, we are reclaiming that power. Recognizing that our emotions are a personal responsibility gives us a strong foundation for reclaiming that power.

Drawing off our earlier chapters about the SuperLoop and RespondAbility, individual leadership allows us to have more agency in how we allow the circumstances around us to affect us. This isn't to say that the circumstances around us are entirely in our control, that we are responsible for managing the bad behavior of others, or that someone or something inflicting trauma or harm needs to be ignored or "soldiered through." What it does mean is that we must have a committed practice to process our own emotions while also honoring the commitments we've made as part of our profession. It is not the responsibility of our teammates, our partners, our parents, or our bosses to handle our emotions. Emotions are signals from our SuperLoop that our body and mind are responding to something in ourselves, in another person, or in our environment—and those emotions are meant to be processed and addressed. We have a responsibility to address those emotions as part of being an effective professional and human.

This, like all competencies, takes time to develop. The practices discussed in this chapter will allow an individual, team, and organization to cultivate their ability to respond rather than react. The power that consciousness can grant us is immense. Our RespondAbility reclaims our agency where others might see themselves as powerless.

RESPONDING UNDER FIRE

HUMAN VIBE: "LIFE IS HAPPENING FOR ME RATHER THAN TO ME." Life is not something that is inflicted upon an individual but rather something that they engage with constantly. The idea that something is happening "to" an individual is a type of accepted powerlessness. Although we cannot control all aspects of life, we want to own aspects that are indeed within our control and influence.

Senator Diana DiZoglio was able to weather the challenges she faced because of her ability to respond, her sense of responsibility, and her determination to lead. This, ultimately, benefited people who weren't her.

In 2017, Diana was undertaking the huge task of addressing the harassment and silencing of Senate aides and junior legislators. Diana, who had herself been harassed as a young legislator, entered a session that was hostile to her and weathered the kinds of accusations, recriminations, and questioning that many victims of sexual harassment and assault are forced to endure from society. After defending the need for transparency in settlements by the state, Diana was exhausted and shaken.

She left her seat for a moment to gather her things and found a simple note that had been left anonymously on her chair.

The message read "Thank you," and it went on to detail that this person, who was a legislative aide, the position Diana had previously occupied, was dealing with the same issues as Diana. They just didn't have the power or position to step forward.

Diana's ability to engage with her responsibility rather than with her knee-jerk reactions is at the core of Operationalizing our consciousnesses. It allowed her to achieve great strides for the people of her state because it's at the core of great responsibility and leadership. It's something that all of us can strive for in our work and our leadership to unlock our full potential.

As of 2024, Diana continues to represent her constituents and fight the good fight for those who are committed to transparency and accountability.

"Do the best you can until you know better.
Then when you know better, do better."

—Oprah Winfrey on Maya Angelou[44]

CHAPTER SIX

HUMANCENTRIC ORGANIZATIONS

I n the early 2000s, I was in my twentieth year as the founding CEO of Little Sprouts Child Enrichment Schools, focused on infants through school-age children, committed to meeting the educational milestones and, most importantly, the social and emotional skills needed to thrive in system-impacted communities. It was my first business that I began at seventeen, and it is currently owned by Babilou, a global network of 1,100 early education and care schools operating in twelve countries and serving more than 50,000 families. The years I spent building Little Sprouts are where I evolved many of the principles that would ultimately lead to the founding of G3 and the creation of the SuperLoop and Praxis concepts. In an era that is already one of my most treasured, I can safely say that one of the more important moments in my professional life, and in the development of Little Sprouts, was when we won the contract

---

44 Oprah Winfrey summarized the ideas of Maya Angelou on her May 12, 2013, episode of *The Oprah Winfrey Show*.

to work with Roxbury Community College and become the center of their early childhood development lab program, where students would work as teaching assistants and interns.

This era and this contract with Roxbury Community College were critically important to my development as a leader because they offered the opportunity for me to understand so much about relating to people and the forces at work within communities and organizations—both those that are commonly discussed and talked about and those that we ignore or overlook. Roxbury is a historically Black neighborhood, one that has a rich history and a strong community. Roxbury is the home of Crispus Attucks, who is heralded as the first Black American killed in the Revolutionary War when they were shot during the Boston Massacre. Malcom X, Dr. Martin Luther King Jr., Coretta Scott King, Sylvia Plath, and Mel King have all contributed to the cultural tapestry of Roxbury, which is a place that has always been at the forefront of the fight for equity. It's a community that has all the benefits of being an old, storied neighborhood but one that also suffers from the impacts of institutional racism and systemic neglect. This meant that Little Sprouts would have to find a way to benefit from the historic strength of Roxbury's society while also engaging with the challenges it was facing.

One of the biggest programs Little Sprouts undertook was the Early Reading First (ERF) project, part of the No Child Left Behind (NCLB) federal initiative begun in 2001. The ERF invested $10 billion aimed at increasing literacy by providing funding and curriculum to programs in preschools, particularly those serving low-income communities. Research clearly shows that closing the achievement gap begins in preschool and that family engagement is a huge predictor of literacy and oral language skills, so many of the aspects of the

ERF curriculum were based on, of course, parental involvement.[45, 46] One of the biggest struggles Little Sprouts confronted was that, despite the best intentions of the people who designed them, ERF and NCLB programs created to help student outcomes weren't thoroughly equipped to do so.

We faced a very clear but difficult-to-address challenge—100 percent of the students in Roxbury were considered at risk, and approximately 20 percent of those students had parents who were incarcerated. This meant that, despite the very best of intentions from the well-educated, middle-class intellectuals who designed the program, the parents and children in Roxbury were unlikely to live in the same situation as the hypothetical children for whom the 10B National initiative was designed.

The first years of working with the NCLB program were very successful for the students at Little Sprouts. Despite the fact that Little Sprouts ranked in the top 5 percent of the ERF programs nationally as an institution, it would turn out that there were hidden issues that needed to be addressed. The family engagement practices of ERF didn't bring the even-higher results we expected. The children in the classrooms sometimes weren't able to concentrate because of various home-life challenges—they'd missed breakfast or they'd arrived late. Many of the staff in the program were not consistent in their punctuality and attendance because of transportation difficulties or other responsibilities. Although we were making progress, I knew we could

45   W. Steven Barnett and Cynthia E. Lamy, "7 Achievement Gaps Start Early: Preschool Can Help," *Closing the Opportunity Gap: What America Must Do to Give Every Child an Even Chance* (2013), https://doi.org/10.1093/acprof:oso/9780199982981.003.0007.

46   W. Steven Barnett, "Preschool Education and Its Lasting Effects: Research and Policy Implications," *Boulder and Tempe: Education and the Public Interest Center and Education Policy Research Unit* (2008), http://epicpolicy.org/publication/preschooleducation.

do better. I wanted to see what I could do to amplify the curriculum and reinforce the home-based elements of the ERF program to push our scores even higher. This would all change after I met Mr. George, one of our parents, at a regular Family Round Table, our quarterly nighttime meeting for the parents, teachers, and staff of Little Sprouts.

I still remember this night very well. Roxbury Community College, the campus that housed Little Sprouts, required a long walk from a far-off parking lot that gave me a lot of time to think as I made my way through the dark and into the early childhood school. I knew that the parents would be sitting in the little children's chairs and that the room would be decorated and cute, but there would be plenty of anxiety once I entered the room. Not because of the content of the meeting (which was really a time to pat ourselves on the back and redouble our efforts), but because of who I was and what my identity represented to my parents and students.

I was, no matter my good intentions, an apparent outsider to Roxbury for a variety of reasons. Despite working with the poverty-impacted community of East Roxbury, I was a woman whom the parents at Little Sprouts might think of as wealthy, someone who wore Marc Jacobs outfits and was finally seeing results from building up a number of early education schools. I was one of the few white educators who worked with these families—so much so that they frequently referred to me as "the white lady" in an affectionate manner but also in a way that reminded me of the difference in experiences we'd inevitably have. Although I'd worked hard and sacrificed a lot to build the collection of early education schools, I had never faced many of the challenges that the parents and children in Little Sprouts Roxbury were facing. I'd been aware of all of these factors and had been grappling with them for quite some time, but these truths would become even clearer to me at the round table meeting where I'd meet

Mr. George, who would provide me with a new perception of our school, my role, our students, and our parents—and what it was like to grow up in Roxbury and places like it.

I could hear the parents chattering away as they ate pizza and drank apple juice in the early childhood classroom, but when I stepped in, the room became dead silent. This was going to be a positive meeting for the school, which had many undertones that had to be recognized to understand the perspective of the Roxbury parents at the meeting that night. The classroom was designed to be a place that put you at ease, but it was small, old, and in need of an updated environment. Roxbury Community College is located just down the street from a police station and a county jail, where many of the parents in the classroom that night had friends, relatives, or even spouses incarcerated—mere blocks away right at that moment. The attending parents were sitting in children's chairs, and I was towering above them. I was about to step in front of that classroom and celebrate the accomplishments of the students and reinforce that we should continue to engage in the home-based elements of the ERF program. I was going to be a cheerleader that night, but the mood didn't match what I wanted to provide.

This vibe only got worse as I went into my presentation about the ERF plan to help the parents and students accelerate their learning. I was in front of them, going over the metrics surrounding the school on charts and graphs. Despite the fact that this was celebratory, and all the numbers were great, I could tell that I was losing their attention and that the whole thing seemed remote and distant. As I began to discuss parental involvement elements—reading three new books a week, using new words at home, and other supposedly easy activities parents were meant to undertake—I saw overt dismay on the faces of the parents in front of me. Slowly, only the teachers in the room were engaging with me. I couldn't figure out what was wrong.

Until a parent in his early thirties spoke up from the middle of the room. This was Mr. George.

Despite the obvious weight I could see on his face, he approached the conversation gently. He asked my name again and then asked if he could call me "Miss Susan."

"Miss Susan, I don't know if you know what it's like to work for a shitty boss. To be beaten down for eight or ten hours a day, every day. To try and work yourself out of the situation we're all in around here and to not be able to do it."

He paused, looked at me, and said, "I can barely find it in me to handle day-to-day tasks in my family when I get home. Dinner, homework, baths, and getting ready for the next day. All the while, I'm wondering how I can get my boss to treat me better or if I can somehow get a better first job, yet I also need a second job just to make ends meet."

And then, "Something that sounds so easy, like reading a book … It's basically impossible."

Mr. George stood up and pointed all around the room.

"I don't know if any of us are ever going to get out of this situation, but we work hard at it—and I don't want to walk out of here feeling like a failure as a parent again."

All around the room, I could see parents lighting up and nodding; the energy level suddenly shot up. Despite all the work we put into the environment, it was still a small place with flickering lights. The bathrooms didn't always work. The atmosphere had seemed oppressive a moment ago, but now it seemed as if the room was filled with life as other parents chimed in and began to tell me about their own situations.

I knew right then that if we truly wanted to succeed in accelerating the learning of our children by capturing the energy in this room, we would need to address the needs of our community of students, parents, and teachers. To be an effective service for these groups, we would need to live in the reality of their world. Not our reality, but in theirs.

Mr. George and the other parents there that night showed me that we were, by attempting to follow the surface-level recommendations of the ERF program, ignoring the realities that many of our parents faced. I was part of the problem even though I thought I was bringing solutions.

The key to overcoming the many challenges involved in ERF was to engage with everyone involved with Little Sprouts—teachers, students, parents, and staff—and to ultimately make Little Sprouts into a Humancentric Organization that engaged with all the forces that were affecting these families. We'd need to center our organization on the people who made up the fabric of our communities. The children and parents weren't just people from whom we needed specific results. The teachers weren't just curriculum machines meant to deliver lessons with maximum efficiency. The other staff in the program weren't productivity machines who kept the rooms in order or acted as supervisors. The parents weren't just there to buttress their children's learning, they were there to be parents.

Humancentric Organizations

The night that I met Mr. George, I didn't think that I'd learn something that would revolutionize my already successful schools. All I knew was that I didn't want to walk into another meeting that showed me as disconnected, as privileged, as somebody who was ignorant because I was living a fundamentally easier life. Although I was already aware of all the sum of the challenges that the employees and parents at Little Sprouts were facing, I couldn't really imagine the particular conditions of those challenges until I'd been allowed to consider the human who existed inside of these difficulties. I was ashamed that I hadn't truly seen the whole picture before Mr. George brought it to my attention—but I was aware of the great opportunity this expanded perception offered us. I understood all of this on an intellectual level, but Mr. George had given me the gift of making it real and visceral. He gave me insight into systemic racism and generational inequality in a way that I simply could not expect to understand from my own experiences.

In all transparency, I cried on the way home as I thought about what I'd been missing as these students and parents worked so hard to excel despite everything pressing down on them. How many emotions I was handling; shame, frustration, and despair from the reality that I was adding to the challenges of these parents and teachers rather than creating a better place for love to grow.

Although Mr. George wasn't an employee, it was the consideration of the whole of his humanity that led directly to the changes at Little Sprouts. The intentional changes benefited everyone while increasing organizational effectiveness as we aligned with actualizing our mission. It was my genesis of the concept of a Humancentric Organization (HCO) and was also the first spark that led me to establishing G3 and codifying SuperLoop Praxis.

Humancentric systems are organizations that care for the I level of the organization and therefore receive great benefits to the WE and ALL levels of their operation. Humancentric Organizations see their employees, leadership, and customers as more than mere resources, as whole people in need of community, support systems, satisfaction, and purpose. There is now an entire movement of conscious companies building on the work of Raj Sisodia and John Mackey's pioneering book, *Conscious Capitalism*. On average, HCOs committed to conscious practices like Whole Foods, The Container Store, Tom's Shoes, Athletica, and Eileen Fisher report outperformance of traditional publicly traded companies on the S&P 500 index by 10.5 times.[47]

And why? HCOs treat people at all levels better, and that leads to increased engagement, retention, and productivity. As Dr. Phil Zelazo, leading researcher at University of Minnesota and cofounder of Reflective Performance Inc., highlights, to maximize ROI in systems change requires two fundamental changes: 1) a focus on people as people first, and on their human performance, and 2) a systems-level (as opposed to point-to-point) objective measurement and analysis.[48]

Intentionally developing the people in your organization is more important to its success than traditional employee training—but this is something companies do not often recognize or know how to Operationalize. Treating people, their essential humanity, as being the core pillar of an organization means helping them engage in inside-out work so that they can cultivate, transform, and actualize. This is not only ethical, but it ends in returns on investment because of the quality of work they will produce, the strong fabric it will create for your organization, and the continual growth of the individual, which will have a massive return on the time and resources invested. When the core needs of the employees are met, they can better address the needs of the organization.

---

47   Raj Sisodia, "Companies That Practice 'Conscious Capitalism' Perform Better," *Harvard Business Review*, April 1, 2013, https://hbr.org/2013/04/companies-that-practice-conscious-capitalism-perform.

48   Reflective Performance, "Return on Investment," Reflective Performance Inc., accessed June 6, 2024, https://reflectiveperformanceinc.com/impact/return-on-investment/.

Gallup shows that, since the early seventies, the numbers demonstrate that engagement is steadily dropping. Only 30 percent of employees are highly engaged, 65 percent are not engaged, and 30 percent of those are actively sabotaging because they are so disengaged. So-called "Quiet Quitting" isn't some new phenomenon that can be blamed on Gen Z and millennials or on COVID-19.[49] The crisis of engagement is readily apparent across most American industries, with an annual cost of $60 billion. The only thing that will change such a problem is to address the core issues that are the root cause of this phenomenon.

For Little Sprouts, engaging with the whole person meant recognizing the material conditions surrounding our families, teachers, and students—and allowing people the space and opportunity to bring themselves into a Humancentric Organization that would engage with these material conditions.

To Operationalize the new understanding that Mr. George had provided, Little Sprouts launched into proactive solution mode. We began to record book readings from teachers, that aligned with the books in our take home family libraries, so that students could listen to them at home, rather than being dependent on parents. We made flashcards related to the rare words and created other reading aids parents were now able to use at home as part of the overall interventions. Making these simple, intentional adaptations and allowances changed everything. Soon, these tactics and the positive results they yielded made me realize that there were many places in our structure where we could Operationalize ourselves as a Humancentric Organization.

---

49   Ben Wigert, "Your Employee Engagement Program Isn't Working," Gallup, April 14, 2020, https://www.gallup.com/workplace/308780/employee-engagement-program-isn-working.aspx.

We began to expand our course options for both teachers and families, offering options for mornings, afternoons, nights, and weekends and providing childcare to enable participation without the restriction and cost of a babysitter. Another impediment to engaging with this client and employee development was the sheer amount of time that the families and employees had to spend on finding transportation (because of their lack of access). We began to provide transportation from a local company for several Little Sprouts locations so that families would have more downtime before their students came home (and therefore more energy for their children's education) rather than sitting in traffic or being on public transportation. It is worth noting that this actually presented an additional problem—the only face-to-face time we were able to reliably get with some families was at the moment of pickup or drop-off, and we didn't want to lose this regular interaction by now offering transportation. We solved for this by scheduling weekly one-on-one calls with families. We also continued with our in-person monthly Family Round Table meetings.

All of this benefited our students, which benefited our teachers, which benefited our entire program. It allowed the parents to have meaningful involvement in a way that wasn't denigrating or doomed to failure. Things began to change rapidly, all because I'd had the opportunity to set aside my ego and my thoughts about the way things should be in the face of Mr. George and the other community members who shared their experiences. This was further supplemented by offering take-home meals from a local caterer, which addressed data that inadequate nutrition impacts learning and brain development, relieved some financial stress from families, and gave parents more time and freedom for educational and social learning. We were able to cover 90 percent of this food expense through the Department of Education's food reimbursement program. The step of including dinner was absolutely critical to our process on both a literal and symbolic level. It demonstrated the deep level of commitment from Little Sprouts, the support systems from the state, and the families.

This wasn't charity. I, in fact, almost hate the word "charity" because it implies that the receiving party is deadweight, as if they aren't going to be part of an even stronger community once we've helped them progress or recover. This program wasn't for the sake of goodness, or inspiration, or even from the perspective of pure morality. What was being done here was a direct response to the systemic inequality most (if not all) of our population faced as they attempted to pursue education for their children and themselves, even as they pursued their own careers with the desire to make a better life for their families than they experienced. We, essentially, needed to overcome the barriers placed in front of our students. There was a regular lack of access to food, education, employment, and a functioning justice system for the families at our school. These are all barriers to performance. When our basic needs are not met, there is no certainty of our hard work paying off.

With these barriers removed, everyone involved was offered the opportunity to perform at their best.

We, consequently, had students who were more ready and able to learn both at home and at school. The increased outcomes meant that we could more easily apply for funding and support from outside organizations—the equivalent of having metrics that might bring investment inside the private sector. The programs, while initially looking like pure assistance, ended up benefiting everyone involved because they were really a manifestation of addressing systemic inequality.

HUMAN VIBE: "NOTHING ABOUT US WITHOUT US." This Human Vibe is a reminder that we cannot actively engage with what people need without involving them. Distant academics or isolated C-suite executives do not understand what an individual group needs to prosper because they cannot fully comprehend their lived experience. A priori logic isn't enough to change the world, and we must emphasize Praxis that is inclusive of those impacted.

This embrace of the Humancentric mode of thought also extended to additional investment in our teachers and staff. Many organizations would have considered the early childhood education teachers to be low skill or easily replaced childcare employees. Not only was this not the case at Little Sprouts, but it's also not the case in any educational institution. One thing I noticed as I continued my career in early childhood education was that there was a large turnover rate in early childhood education teachers. This was not only true at the early education level on the East Coast but is true of the entire industry. The turnover rate of lower education (K–12) teachers nationwide is a very high 8 percent annually. A staggering 44 percent of K–12 teachers quit after five years in the profession. This is largely because they do not receive the pay, safety, recognition, developmental support, or material support their jobs require to be done efficiently.[50]

These numbers are considered very high. The numbers for preschool and kindergarten are even higher. Little Sprouts started out

---

50   Jake Bryant, Samvitha Ram, Doug Scott, and Claire Williams, "K–12 Teachers Are Quitting. What Would Make Them Stay?" McKinsey & Company, March 2, 2023, https://www.mckinsey.com/industries/education/our-insights/k-12-teachers-are-quitting-what-would-make-them-stay.

with 40 percent turnover per year, which was average in Massachusetts in 2004, but we ended up with only a 26 percent annual turnover after our transformation. This was one of the biggest reductions across the entire country.

I wanted to combat this rapid turnover at Little Sprouts, so we began to continually reinvest in our teachers with both material support and an Operationalizing of the values we are discussing in the form of Connection Time, learning and development, coaching on performance, and mental and emotional well-being. As I went on to found G3 Works and create the SuperLoop Praxis model, this would form the basis of what would come to be two specific roles known as the Pathmaker (which we'll cover in more detail below) and Performance Coach.

Although these changes and programs might seem very particular to an early childhood education program, they aren't. We spent over twenty years validating this proof of concept in a spectrum of industries. And it worked. Better and better each time. It is because they are changes that embody a Humancentric process that can be Operationalized at any organization. Like many of the innovations related to SuperLoop, these changes begin with a shift in perception and involve addressing the I/WE/ALL of an organization that empowers everyone, leading to increased measurable results and an ability to maximize human potential and performance.

Simply put, we must support the various participants in our business ecology: the customers, leaders, employees, partners, and communities. All of these individuals, if adequately considered, will be empowered to give more and do more. This is where successful Humancentric programs diverge from human-resources-minded companies. We know that time off and Humancentric policies are critical to productivity and individual health, but many business cultures treat their employees as replaceable as often as they see them as something to be cultivated.

The Perils of the Human Commodity— Humans Are Not Just a Resource

The consequences of the practice of using humans as a commodity have become more and more evident. Gallup has identified that 65 percent of workers are disengaged from their work, 50 percent of workers only fulfill their job duties to the letter and not one iota more, and 20 percent of these disengaged people are actively disengaged, and thereby actively sabotaging the efforts of their workplace by taking away from the collective momentum of their organizational mission.[51] As grim as these numbers are, they likely do not account for those who have been left behind by their industries through unemployment or wage stagnation. These companies do not center on the human, and this leads to a shortfall in their missions, losses in productivity, and a loss in motivation and morale on the part of their workers. All of these losses, of course, are represented by financial consequences.

A Humancentric company is very different from a company that is purely human-resources-driven. The difference is evident, even from the terminology. The very vocabulary involved in "human resources" contains the essence of the problem within non–Humancentric Organizations—that they view the humans at their company as a resource to be exploited. In capitalism, we know that resources are there to be acquired, leveraged, and consumed for the sake of profit. Thinking of our team in this mindset will inevitably lead to them, in one way or

---

51   Ben Wigert, "4 Ways to Improve Employee Engagement," Gallup, January 23, 2020, https://www.gallup.com/workplace/285674/improve-employee-engagement-workplace.aspx.

another, being considered consumable. There's an inherent objectification to the term that doesn't serve a company well.

It's no secret to the reading audience of this book that HR departments have become primarily about limiting liability for a company. They are there, in most cases, to act on behalf of the employer rather than the employee. They are, in actuality, meant to maximize the value of an employee to a company over most other concerns. When they encounter a human problem, their solution is usually to make it so that this problem doesn't find its way into the professional setting. If this isolation proves to be impossible, it often results in letting a person go.

As much as the name suggests that the institution is there to act as a resource for employees, it is much more like a department that makes humans into a consumable resource, and this is a problem.

A resource, after all, is gone once you consume it. My company, G3 Works, is the Golden Goose Group—it's named, of course, for the fable of the miraculous goose that is ultimately destroyed because the farmer who discovered it tries to push too many eggs from it. Exploitation consumes the miracle.

The way that a non-Humancentric company consumes its employees is not obvious or even necessarily intentional. It happens by way of the top-down, command-and-control system that discourages the presence of humanity at work. It's something that we usually refer to as "professionalism" or as someone who can "leave it at the door"; it's something that is seen as beneficial to the whole company, but like many of the issues discussed in this book, it is ultimately a debt that has to be paid off, or perhaps a dam that is doomed to burst if it isn't maintained.

THE WORK/LIFE BALANCE LIE

So why do we continue to engage in this unhealthy perception of work and the human role in work?

The concept of work/life balance is at the core of this unhealthy view of people. It suggests that work is a place that is independent of the rest of our existence. If we try to live in this concept, we are expected to shelve the rest of our lives when we enter work and to shelve work when we return home. This firewall is meant to be impermeable—which means that any time our home life enters work, we are engaging in a breach of professionalism. This systemically reinforces the idea that problems that don't seem to relate directly to our work role (like those that were being faced at Little Sprouts) are not to be discussed in a professional setting. It also, as a convenient byproduct, keeps people from discussing the inadequacies of what an organization provides for its dedicated employees. We can't discuss the consequences of low compensation or poor benefits—to do so is "unprofessional." The idea that our personal lives shouldn't enter the workspace keeps an organization from having to deal with the consequences of many of its policies ranging from poor benefits or compensation to a toxic culture or poor leadership. This prohibition against such discussions keeps the system from ever changing. There is no Mr. George to expose the actuality of these situations because Mr. George would be fired or disciplined. Nobody will make the same demands for change as Mr. George because to do so would be too risky.

In many cases, this "firewall," this expected barrier between a "work-life" and a "personal life," results in encouraging the symptoms of workaholism, aka the hustle and grind culture, a situation where we work to shut out the personal life we've been trained to neglect for most of our waking day. I include myself in this; for years, I had to retrain myself not to feel guilty if I wasn't thinking about work for almost every waking moment or if I was thinking about my boys when I was working.

This is the kind of mindset that can lead us to treat ourselves or our employees as if they are consumable resources rather than human beings.

There are signs that a company is treating their employees as commodities, which means that it will be impacted by this practice that has serious consequences on the WE/ALL level that manifest in the ways I've described above. These practices often show up as an expectation that a worker will neglect their personal life or sacrifice their health on (what's believed to be) behalf of the company.

One sign of a company that commodifies its humans is the presence of little to no parental leave. Parenting is something that is impossible to simply "leave at home," and trying to do so will have a permanent impact on a child—which will ultimately result in an impact on an employee. A similar metric exists in PTO. Companies that commodify humans will have little to no PTO or expect employees to take unpaid leave when they have a human need. This inherently puts both health and personal life in an adversarial position with the employer, and PTO is directly tied to job satisfaction. According to a 2018 Society for Human Resource Management (SHRM) article, a rise in PTO taken tends to tie into increases in productivity directly. Seventy-eight percent of supervisors surveyed by Project: Time Off indicated that paid time off and vacation improved employee focus, and 81 percent indicated that their experience showed that time off curtailed burnout.[52]

---

52 Stephen Miller, "Workers Are Taking More Vacation Time, but It's Not Enough," SHRM, March 4, 2020, https://www.shrm.org/resourcesandtools/hr-topics/employee-relations/pages/workers-taking-more-vacation-.aspx.

None of this is to say that material results aren't expected from employees in a Humancentric system. *We are—as professionals—not getting paid to just "work hard"; rather, we are paid to get results*, not to merely exist or be present. I'm not suggesting that work be a big therapy session or that a company is responsible for the entire personal lives of those in the organization.

We can't write off our responsibilities because of other aspects of our lives—"I didn't accomplish my deliverables because I'm distracted at work/home."

> **We don't get paid to work hard; we get paid to get results.**

Instead, we can stay transparent and honor our responsibilities while still engaging with our whole persons—"Hey, all, I'm acknowledging I am distracted today as I have X going on. You can count on me to get X done or I get to renegotiate X deliverables to be complete by next Tuesday rather than Friday. Can we make that work?"

What I am establishing is that ignoring these elements of the I, ignoring the Humancentric, is wildly unrealistic. The aspects, strengths and weaknesses, light and shadow, of the person that the Humancentric model addresses and nurtures will come through. We're human; it has to be.

Companies have many reasons they claim that they can't enact these sorts of practices. I've heard it all—"We can't do this because it costs too much," or "This isn't the role of the workplace"—but turnover is more expensive, and the loss of productivity is too costly to ignore. Gallup research has found that there are $450 to $550 billion in losses in the US each year from a lack of engagement and a consequent loss in productivity. Ironically, the same companies that do not want to engage in cultural development and a deliberately developmental design will cite the cost of these efforts as one of the reasons they do not change.

Every year that this lack of engagement isn't addressed is a further loss. Strong companies simply cannot afford to pretend that the dissatisfaction of their employees does not have material costs. If these losses were from a different aspect of a business—such as in their sales—a failure to address such a problem would be blatant incompetence. However, because this area has been culturally neglected, we believe that we do not have the tools to directly address these impacts on retention, recruiting, and turnover.

An awareness of our emotions is a skill set in the managerial toolbox and creates the workforce climate as much as (I'd suggest perhaps even more so) than leadership and operational skills management.

As the great John Mackey, founder of Whole Foods, says, "Love belongs back in the workplace."[53] Love is a verb as well as a noun. So how do we create the practice of love at work?

Imagine a company with minimal turnover. Imagine rarely having to train new employees because the entire work environment is designed for continuous improvement of the existing workforce. (Dr. W. Edwards Deming popularized his work in Japan with Kaizen—"change for the better"—creating total quality management [TQM] which was focused primarily on processes, products, and services rather than human development.) Imagine employees who deliver the results of career-long training and development that's been buttressed by very high levels of satisfaction. The benefits are too great to ignore.

It's the very best of both the employee and the organization, and it unlocks the kinds of possibilities that simply aren't present in a

53   John Mackey, "Lead with Love," John Mackey, February 14, 2023, https://johnpmackey.com/lead-with-love/.

flawed, unbalanced system of individuals who are unmotivated or exploited.

So how do we get there?

Operationalizing a Humancentric Methodology

The opportunity for growth and mentorship is critical to a Humancentric company and to Operationalizing Consciousness. Consequently, part of the SuperLoop Praxis is engaging with a new role and mindset, the Pathmaker.

The Pathmaker position is specifically designed to work with employees to access support as they continue to grow in their roles. Pathmakers address the whole person aspects of an organization and seek to reinforce meaning, purpose, and satisfaction by facilitating the advancement and engagement of the whole human.

The Pathmaker is the facilitator connecting an individual to the services that they need to move their potential into high performance. HR is about codifying the individual, while the Pathmaker is about situational awareness. In terms of function, the role is a mix of life coach and social worker who moves their peers forward. Pathmakers use scheduled, regular Connection Times to measure employee growth and to plan to break through the barriers to high performance these individuals are experiencing. They utilize the cooperation of performance coaches, executives, and others to maximize the performance of those they serve as part of their role.

The Pathmaker focuses on the five elements of well-being as defined by Gallup—career, social, financial, physical, and community well-being.[54] People are conditioned not to talk about being system-impacted because they get stratified into those groups, and the system does not reach out to lower-stratified individuals. The Pathmaker role normalizes the support systems a human needs and optimizes human potential and organizational performance.

Using Pathmakers, Little Sprouts implemented the Rising Sprouts program, which was a mentorship program designed to help employees move up within the company. As part of the program, there was an increase in classroom coaching, which provided mentees with the skills they would require to thrive in their current role while also moving toward their futures. Rising Sprouts mentees were first trained in the skills they needed to perform their jobs successfully. After that, on-the-job coaching was used to help mentees model and apply the skills they learned in the classroom. This process required role practice, which involved doing two to three repetitions of the skills before doing them in a live, practical setting. The program was based on the apprenticeship model; it is both collaborative and shaped toward the individual, meaning that participatory learning was emphasized over an authority-centered approach. This allowed mentees to cocreate a world that works for everyone—which eventually became the G3 tagline.

Any company can create a Pathmaker system to help employees engage with support and create upward mobility. Although the Pathmaker role provides amazing benefits as a "secretary of cultural development," the Pathmaker doesn't need to be a full-time role—it can also be an external strategic partner, part of another leadership role, as well as a set of values that is reinforced by policy, material

54 Tom Rath and Jim Harter, "The Five Essential Elements of Well-Being," Gallup, accessed June 6, 2024, https://www.gallup.com/workplace/237020/five-essential-elements.aspx.

support, and a consistent, driven effort toward whole person improvement for the benefit of everyone.

CREATING A HUMANCENTRIC ENVIRONMENT

Companies can engineer their spaces to make them more friendly to the whole person. A truly Humancentric Organization will look toward the needs of employees—cocreated with employees—to reap the benefits of this system and create an equitable relationship between employer and employee. Studies have found that both lean office spaces (where there is tight control over "extras" in the office) and "enriched" office spaces (those with a large number of amenities that go beyond the norm) hurt productivity and morale for various reasons. What was shown to benefit employees' psychological state and productivity the most is when office spaces are reflective of the desires and needs of employees and defined by a knowledge of these needs rather than an institutional solution.[55]

In Little Sprouts, this manifested as responsive changes that dealt deliberately with the needs of employees. In response to the high stress of childhood education, we offered a chair massage program that had been created by a former employee, my beloved friend Donna. We also offered nutrition, yoga, resistance classes, and optional services for work and home. These were also important because they were based on direct requests from team members.

The children and employees engaged in meditation, and children were able to get kid-oriented massages and to engage in body and brain well-being exercises. Since these programs were so successful,

---

55   Craig Knight and S. Alexander Haslam, "The Relative Merits of Lean, Enriched, and Empowered Offices: An Experimental Examination of the Impact of Workspace Management Strategies on Well-Being and Productivity," *Journal of Experimental Psychology: Applied* 16, no. 2 (June 2010): 158–72, https://doi.org/10.1037/a0019292.

the school began to engage in aromatherapy and music as further steps toward lowering the stress levels while increasing the level of engagement. The music was upbeat and engaging, dealing with revolutionary subject matter that was relevant to the families in the communities we served. Based on studies on teaching environments, we also changed the light bulbs to be more reminiscent of natural light and removed discordant notes from classrooms by replacing loud pieces of equipment. In a move that was against common knowledge at the time (but one that would ultimately be adopted by the wider community), our teachers created a policy to have only 25–30 percent of wall space covered to avoid overstimulation for students and faculty. We adopted language that encouraged agency rather than empty praise to ensure we stimulated executive function skills. We designed table and chair spaces to be "problem-solving areas" that invited children to practice Healthy Conflict when there were interpersonal or behavioral issues.

It's worth noting that this process goes beyond just providing physical accommodations that deal with comfort and moves into addressing the aspects of workspaces and behaviors that have historically been neglected by leadership in command-and-control style companies.

HOW LEARNING AND DEVELOPMENT CREATE ENGAGEMENT

One of the most critical aspects of running a successful organization is finding the meaning and engagement we found at Little Sprouts—the type of meaning and engagement I would later activate throughout G3. Studies by Gallup examined why employee engagement programs often fail to improve employee performance and satisfaction, despite being widely used by many organizations. They found that employee engagement is more than just a training program or initiative. In fact, at G3 our motto is "training doesn't work," which may seem curious since we are a learning and development organization. What we have learned over time is that the "training of the month" approach that is utilized by many corporations is simply not integrated with meaningful support, implementation, measurement, and a collaborative strategic plan. This empty training actually fatigues and frustrates team members rather than increasing performance.

Unlike a once-per-year training course, effective learning and development is an ongoing process that requires a continuous measurement of employees' needs and specific project plans committed to making meaningful changes in the organization's culture and management practices. Humancentric companies engage with this as a strategic priority rather than optics as a matter of optics. Too often, training in DEI has become an ineffectual exercise in placation or liability management rather than the ongoing commitment it should be. Budget, resources, and time are necessary to maximize the benefits of an engaged employee by integrating deliberately developmental design elements, thus ensuring personal growth is a core practice of the company. Consistent dosage and high repetitions is how we invest in new learning to maximize impact.

Gallup further found that most employee engagement programs fail because they are focused on superficial fixes rather than addressing the underlying causes of low engagement. Many programs rely too heavily on flawed surveys or other methods of gathering data. They further fail by not providing meaningful follow-up actions or keeping in communication with employees to enact Humancentric initiatives.[56] Employees become disenchanted and disengaged when there is a lack of commitment on the side of the organization.

Simply put, the values in a company need to be lived and experienced on an individual and collective level. They can't just be top-down commands and an inspirational quote that's stuck to the wall. Organizational development is as fundamental to the success of a business as other critical divisions like HR, operations, or finance are.

HUMAN VIBE: "PEOPLE SUPPORT WHAT THEY HELP CREATE." Clarity and collaboration create buy-in. Leaders cannot create in a vacuum. Employees must feel like their talents are being utilized and developed effectively. Nothing can be done in a Humancentric way without the presence of those who know their situation best—"nothing about us without us."

Successful learning and development programs involve ongoing, iterative engagement with employees. These programs involve cross-sectional team members in the design process and focus on building practices that elevate relationships, trust, and shared accountability. This creates an environment for employees to use their skills and experience and makes the acquisition of new skills something more important than mere training, which can sometimes be seen as just "one more thing to do."

56   Ben Wigert, "Your Employee Engagement Program Isn't Working," Gallup, April 14, 2020, https://www.gallup.com/workplace/308780/employee-engagement-program-isn-working.aspx.

Operationalizing a Humancentric methodology involves learning development, financial and operational prioritization, and mentorship and coaching from a Pathmaker who leads individuals through this development. An organization that offers continual opportunities for growth, a safety net for the employees, and flexibility for the actual lives of their employees, is an organization that retains its people while these very same employees are *providing more value* because they aren't being sabotaged by neglecting their humanity.

I have always seen operating a business as an agreement, even a sacred agreement. Hiring an employee is a promise to provide value for those who provide value for you (and for each other). Breaking this agreement is a systemic problem that affects everyone and ultimately destabilizes our future and throttles our results. As the leaders of the ALL, the organization, we should not exploit and over-leverage employees just because we hold the power of a job and a paycheck over them.

On the other side of this agreement are the employees, who agree to the job descriptions and deliverables they were hired to achieve. If they do not achieve those goals due to malingering or self-sabotage, they are exploiting the trust placed in them during hiring. When this sacred agreement is honored by both parties, it creates integrity and workability. As conscious organizations, we can be good for the world and profit all at once. These Humancentric methods make this path practical.

A company's role is to Operationalize the theoretical and make it practical. The realm of education is about teaching systems, and the professional realm is about teaching skills and competencies needed to actualize these systems in day-to-day practice. Many of those who are disengaged or isolated are in such a state because they don't have access to systems that will teach them the practical, day-to-day competencies to be effective in their role and to apply their strengths and skills in a way that benefits both themselves and their company. Work environments need to be set up as communities of continual learning—which also means they become places of ever-increasing results.

Businesses as Communities of Practice

The opportunity for growth and development is critical in Humancentric Organizations. Many companies engage with professional development (PD), but these are often considered from the perspective of the company only—What does the company need to extract value from the employee? How can the skill set of an individual be leveraged for the whole?

What we want to be asking is: How do we create a learning environment that accesses the human potential of each employee while also increasing value for the entire organization? How can we focus on the strategic goals, values, mission, and vision while also building up our skills and engagement?

A Humancentric Organization ensures its professional development plans are based on the needs of the employee *in addition to* those of the company. Unlike a traditional "human resources" company, a Humancentric company is Operationalizing around the fact that they must develop the whole human to get a better employee—and that this practice is of benefit to the entire I/WE/ALL of an organization.

Establishing development that's also of value to the employee gives a sense of agency. The morale, intention, and commitment of an individual who is pursuing PD is greatly increased when their need for purpose and agency is being addressed. The Gallup evaluation of employee engagement shows that these areas are critical to effectiveness. Employees who have had meaningful interactions with their managers about their goals are almost three times as likely to be engaged employees. This is immediately evident in metrics like retention and advancement.[57]

Similar to the program I would later undertake with The Body Shop, I hired employees with willing enthusiasm and values that aligned with Little Sprouts despite their formal education not necessarily fitting the positions. As time progressed, Little Sprouts helped employees become adjunct professors in the education departments of multiple colleges and grow their knowledge base while expanding the SuperLoop methodology at other institutions throughout Massachusetts with a focus on system-impacted areas. The more goal-driven development we applied at Little Sprouts, the higher our retention became in comparison to the rapid turnover rate of the early education ecosystem. This meant that we spent less time and money on recruiting, conflict resolution, and retraining and gained more value from these employees by increasing competencies and creating internal upskilling with transferable skills.

Employee development is also important for institutional effectiveness. Employers should become aware of the fact that a degree will not provide workplace competencies—that's the onus of the companies. Too many of my colleagues at high levels of leadership expect that recent college graduates will step into their companies with a vast array of skills that they can apply to practical tasks. In reality, college degrees and some certifications are to teach systems of learning and theories or theoretical models—not to teach the specific skills of a fully trained professional with experience.

We have to get real with the fact that, as executives, our responsibility is to teach our new and incumbent employees the day-to-day

---

57   "How to Improve Employee Engagement in the Workplace," Gallup, accessed March 30, 2024, https://www.gallup.com/workplace/285674/improve-employeeengage-ment- workplace.aspx#ite-357506..

skills that will maximize their performance in the businesses we've created—and that this teaching and development becomes a form of compensation that isn't offered by many companies. This truth, if communicated properly to prospective hires, becomes a huge differentiator in recruiting talent.

These considerations are another place where the role of the Pathmaker comes into play. The Pathmaker cultivates these competencies in a way that traditional education and employee development won't. This is a dedicated role that goes beyond onboarding or initial training—people need to be guided through their acquisition of competencies. Having a Pathmaker aligned with coaches and mentors synthesizes talent and competencies with the acquisition of practical skills.

The Pathmaker creates a better culture. The word "culture" comes from "cultivate." Without cultivation, we'll have a barren culture. Not cultivating specific results in our company is like letting a garden grow wild. Rather than a beautifully tended garden, we'll be left with the random accidents that survived despite the lack of care we provided. One of the G3 Human Vibes captures the essence of this: "We get the culture we deserve—by default or design." If we don't plan our culture and manage it, we can't plan and manage the results of that culture. A planned culture will have planned results, a random, haphazard culture will have random, haphazard results.

At Little Sprouts, the Pathmaker role contributed to a rise in productivity in the form of ever-increasing educational metrics. Our Pathmakers used their role to support their fellow employees by cultivating relationships, designing professional development plans, and implementing coaching of students, teachers, and management. As the Pathmaker, coaching, and mentor activities increased in effectiveness with our entry-level employees and first-year educators, the previously mentioned retention rate was double that of comparable teaching institutions in Massachusetts.

This shift for the better is something that always occurs when we ensure we are tending to the Humancentric elements of our company because the increased engagement and lessened cost of turnover lead to a more stable, more knowledgeable organization. This process might seem daunting when it comes to providing this kind of unconventional support for entry-level employees, but there are several ways we can tackle these needs with the support of a Pathmaker and some new thinking around how companies can support their employees to the benefit of everyone.

Operationalizing Material Support

The foundation of Maslow's Hierarchy of Needs is a framework that defines physiological needs as the very foundation of our physical existence as a human: food, water, shelter, clothing, sleep, and breathing.[58] An employee who cannot meet the basic material conditions for flourishing will inherently not perform as well as they would with their needs met. A professional can't be at their best if their need for food, shelter, transportation, and other material items is at risk or absent. Although this may not be as impactful an issue for employees on the management level, almost every company has entry-level and support employees who likely spend a significant amount of time addressing shortfalls in these areas or hiding these realities from their coworkers and supervisors. This was the lesson I learned that night at Roxbury Community College by listening to Mr. George. Not only was he not feeling successful as a working parent, but it was

---

58   Robert J. Taormina and Jennifer H. Gao, "Maslow and the Motivation Hierarchy: Measuring Satisfaction of the Needs," *American Journal of Psychology* 126, no. 2 (2013): 155–77, https://doi.org/10.5406/amerjpsyc.126.2.0155.

also perpetuated by having to constantly be in an unsupportive work environment that was not tuned into the challenges Mr. George (and people like Mr. George) faced as he tried to make ends meet.

I identified, right away, that our team at that school, being from the same community, was also experiencing some of these fundamental life challenges. Not having reliable transportation, for instance, is a critical issue—but it's also one that is considered irresponsible or unprofessional despite the fact that nobody willfully inflicts this situation upon themselves.

Little Sprouts had an excellent potential educator named Gwenda who, as it turned out, did not have a reliable way of getting to work. Despite her strong performance and the enthusiasm to join the team she expressed during her working interview, Gwenda declined accepting the full-time position we offered her.

When I called to ask her why she was not accepting the position, she initially responded that she was having challenges and it wasn't the right time for her to take the job.

"Tell me what kind of challenges and let's see if we can make this work." At first, Gwenda clearly wanted to hide her lack of a reliable car that would get her to all schools across the state because she did not want to appear unprofessional or unreliable.

When I'd spoken to her a while, Gwenda finally shared that her car had been working when she'd applied for the position and completed the interview, but that it was now broken down. The mechanic had told her it was not worth repairing. Worst of all, she simply didn't have the money to buy another car.

Then, in a moment that struck me as particularly tragic, she apologized for wasting my time.

I knew that Gwenda, if she had the opportunity, would be essential to the organization (she would, in fact, work in *all* of our locations as a music therapist), and I didn't want to lose her. During her interview, I had watched her light up a classroom, dynamically engaging with both the children and her fellow teachers.

I knew all the research that stated that live music is one of the most effective ways to increase brain development that impacted literacy and STEM scores in addition to increased well-being. I also knew we could not outright buy her a car; however, her situation inspired us to create a loan program for employees who needed to finance transportation. Gwenda was able to purchase a car and successfully pay us back over a two-year period. Her presence was made completely reliable and within her control; she was still deeply invested in the institution, and the entire community benefited from our Actionable Awareness of her as a complete person.

Our efforts to support our employees and students made us integral in our ecosystem and ensured that people across Roxbury supported us. This program was eventually expanded to all of our locations to great effect. The families that had more face-to-face time rather than spending time doing chores and cooking meals (or being hungry) were the families that were able to focus on take-home literacy programs. These families performed better on tests, and those stronger results create not only communities of belonging, but also more funding opportunities for the schools. The innovations we created, which might appear above and beyond the role of an employer to an outsider, were, in reality, investments that benefited everyone and addressed problems that could not be ignored—especially those that were hurting our ability to grow and flourish because we were neglecting basic needs of humans.

This model of value expansion isn't easily understood by people who are stuck in the mindset of value extraction. When Little Sprouts opened up to outside investment, many VC and strategic partners were initially resistant to these elements as "not being part of our core business" because these benefits were mischaracterized as inefficiencies and a distraction when they actually provided a greater level of productivity from employees, students, and families that ultimately increased the effectiveness and loyalty to the entire brand. Brand loyalty that led to reduced marketing costs since we now had built in brand ambassadors and an increase in customer lifetime value by not only staying with our services for the fourteen years of care for the child. In addition to this incredible commitment, these fourteen-year-olds frequently became counselors in training (CITs) at our camps and subsequently, an average 27 percent of graduating students eventually became teachers in our schools. How about that as a brilliant recruiting strategy?

This model we used at Little Sprouts is not just impactful in early education. We have used SuperLoop Praxis in healthcare, technology, media, hospitality, food service, construction, and retail (just to name a few of the industries we grew into). The key is to Operationalize your organizational priorities so that it benefits the employees—and thus reduces turnover as it increases satisfaction and engagement—the key is to engage with the whole human, working with the individual needs of that employee's life like it matters. Because it does. These processes make us able to build relevant and thriving businesses while contributing to strong public health.

Even if a company does not have employees with material needs at the level of food, shelter, and transportation, it can provide many material assets that are helpful to almost any organization. Providing the appropriate technology, software, or equipment for a task, for instance, can create value for everyone involved in a business—continually progressing employee skill sets and organizational innovation. And I promise you, even your senior managers and executives are dealing with life issues that you may have no clue about until you begin to normalize the practice of bringing the whole human to work.

Pathmakers leaned into this opportunity to support access to digital literacy and technology through partners or their own programs. We currently partner with a nonprofit named Tech Goes Home, an organization that trains students and faculty on how to use educational tablets. GBH (an East Coast public broadcasting station and the largest producer of educational media globally) and the Center for Public Broadcasting combined resources with funding from the NIH to create these programs and acquire the equipment (and keep it updated), as well as provide access to an internet connection. Even as these practices created value for Little Sprouts, they also had a lasting value for the teachers, the parents, and the students.

This is yet another program that might look like charity to an outsider, but one that actually helped the bottom line of our for-profit company while also doing the right thing and building up the actual humans who were stakeholders in our organization.

If we are able to change our mindsets and commit to being Humancentric, we business leaders can provide technology, resources, and the accompanying knowledge to increase employee agency, employee skill sets, and productivity while also acting in a conscious capacity. We can be good humans by operating good businesses.

Capitalism doesn't have to be a zero-sum game—and in fact, it maximizes results when it's a partnership that benefits everyone.

The Path That Sprouts Made

Using a Humancentric model for Little Sprouts had an astonishing impact on the organization. The schools were able to continually expand because of the stability and achievement provided by this style of innovation. I eventually negotiated an acquisition by AEG (American Educational Group) for $5.5 million, and then four years later for $12.5 million. By 2024, Little Sprouts had expanded to provide educational services in more than seventy locations across the Eastern United States while acquiring multiple brands in the process.

To this day, I am still contacted by former students, parents, and teachers from Little Sprouts who thank me for giving them the space to grow. Every "thank you" makes me think of Mr. George and how listening to his desire for us to be unique and deal with the whole human inspired us to a kind of innovation that has led to so much success for so many companies.

"Culture does not make people. People make culture. If it is true that the full humanity of women is not our culture, then we can and must make it our culture."

—CHI AMANDA NGOZI ADICHIE

CHAPTER SEVEN

CULTURE: WHAT IS IT?

Culture is a term we hear often. It feels like an elusive term even after forty years of working with companies that have spent a great amount of capital and time trying to pin down what their culture means. At G3, we define culture as a pattern of behavior we have normalized. It is the personality of the organization. It is the Unsaid, "This is who we are, and this is what we do around here." It is what we do and not what we say we will do. Culture is where all the tools of inside-out work manifests. Our culture is inevitably an expression of what we do, what we believe, and the results we achieve. In the G3 model, culture is a commitment to results, accountability, and upholding values. It is making and keeping commitments.

The G3 model, by starting out at the individual levels of the SuperLoop and practicing Actionable Awareness of our beliefs, biology, and behavior, is able to create and recreate culture through every level of the I/WE/ALL. At G3, we believe that "we get the culture we deserve." Culture is not "out there"; it is "in here." *We are culture.* It begins with our integrity to our word. Nothing works without integrity, and that begins with being "count-on-able." *Can others count on you? Can you count on yourself?*

The problem for many organizations is that much of culture happens by default rather than by design. The tools, practices, and concepts discussed in the previous chapters of this book are the tools that create strong, conscious cultures capable of demonstrating their values in a directed fashion. *What are you willing to do to create the culture of your dreams?*

If a culture is conscious, starting on the individual level where our practices include responsibility for our beliefs, our perception, our biology, our capacity for leadership, our ability to respond, and our honoring of the whole human in the workplace, we create an environment that will inevitably be stronger because it is deliberately designed to be so.

Our Relationships with Ourselves and Others Create Our Culture

Culture is an element of an organization that is all about relationships—our relationships to each other, the relationships between the C-suite and their reports, and the organization's relationship to a larger world. Relationships take time to cultivate, and once they're cultivated, they transform gradually with consistency and new actions. As one of our core Human Vibes says, "No new action, no new results."

Because of this, this is a practice that takes intention, attention, time, diligence, reflection, and repetition. Plan-Do-Reflect-Act (PDRA) is a tool used in many systems. The reflection or the debrief is where the juicy learning comes to life. Humans are social beings and therefore learn best socially and reinforce it with those around us. This chapter will explain how the G3 methodology views organizational culture, how culture affects the I/WE/ALL levels of an organization, and how practices can positively and negatively affect our organizational cultures.

One of my experiences that best underscores some of the many ways we are impacted by the culture within our organization is an experience I had in 2011 with the American Education Group (AEG at the time. It is now named Fusion Group). I sold the majority of my first company, Little Sprouts, to AEG and stayed on as president of my division while I sat on the C-suite executive team leading up organizational development for the entirety of the acquisitions of five brands with more than 2,500 team members.

My initial interest in selling a piece of Little Sprouts was to "learn what I don't know." At this point in my career, I had only worked for myself, and I wanted to work alongside a world-class team committed to creating academic excellence. In this larger role, we would be expanding nationally and learning best practices regarding these ideals. The board and leadership at AEG aligned with our vision, mission, and core values. However, as my team and I would all learn, the power to pivot and create larger impact was controlled by the board of investors, not those of us in leadership positions.

Pete Ruppert was the CEO of AEG. It really was love at first sight, not only with Pete but also with his team that included Jeff, Jenny, Todd, and Steve. The larger strategic plan was to spread my vision and operational practices of a conscious company to an even wider platform. It would allow us to scale and create national impact. When I sold Little Sprouts, I was assured over and over that this company would implement the programs at Little Sprouts in a widespread fashion. It did occur for the first few years. I attended monthly board meetings in Grand Rapids, Michigan, while working with the founder of Fusion Academy, Michelle Rose Gilman, as our most recent acquisition, to expand these practices of SuperLoop throughout our entire business model. Pete and the AEG team introduced us to many fabulous practices that I integrated into the overarching model. Two of the best practices Pete trained us on were Jack Daly's Hyper Sales Growth model (which I credit for creating the 225 percent growth in four years from February 2008 to June 2012—including 2008 when the market crashed and the recession occurred) and Verne Harnish's Scaling Up model, both of which we still use today.

As time went on, however, I increasingly noticed that the efforts that our new company made toward workforce development, training in new practices, and consideration of the whole human were waning as handling multiple major priorities in a fast-growth environment was complex.

Instead of the deliberately developmental organization I'd been hoping for, the acquisition machine took over, and the traditional elements of hierarchy became our priorities. The leadership answered to the board, and the current chairman of the board had a top-down, command-and-control style that had no hope of keeping the community-building and conscious programs that were yielding such results in my organizations. The quality of the education began to change. Like many nonconscious organizations, our focus was centered more on quantity than quality, and employee retention and satisfaction began to wane. This, in turn, started to affect the bottom line.

Do not mistake this comment as "touchy-feely stuff." One of the central Human Vibes in the Golden Goose Group is "no margin, no mission." We cannot operate good businesses without solid and reliable revenue. However, if we do not invest in the ongoing development of the people who bring that vision, mission, and values to life, then the quality suffers. Once the customers become aware of this, the brand suffers, and then you are dealing with your reputation and potential PR nightmares. This is especially true in the care industries with the reality of social media and sites such as Glassdoor (where employees rate their employers). We can no longer promise our employees a transparent culture and then not deliver. The reality of technology is that transparency is going to be either embraced or inflicted.

As part of my role leading organizational development, I recommended we use a 360-degree assessment tool to measure the entire workforce across brands and share the results to create the operational development plan for the next three to five years. Pete and the entire AEG team were enthusiastic and aligned. I personally led the execution as it required training the executive and senior management team as well as support for deploying it throughout the organizations. There was apprehension from some team members regarding the transparency of the process—specifically in the questions requesting anecdotal responses from employees across the organization. "How do we know we will not get backlash from being honest?"

I assured them that they needed to trust the process and that the final aggregate report would be shared company wide and would not have names or any identifying information of those who responded. We highly encouraged all to share their reports with their teams and supervisors but noted this would be an individual choice. It was and still is my belief that both courage and consideration are a practice and the foundations of building trust. We get to be both when giving and receiving FeedForward. I encouraged all of them to be as direct and transparent as possible.

FEEDFORWARD

FEEDFORWARD

FEEDBACK

- - - - - **vs.** - - - - -

The process of sharing perspectives, 1 to 1 and collectively, communicating via a series of strategic questions called Curious Questions.

Presenting another person with a piece of information that pushes them backward.

- -

FeedForward uses three prompts:

1 *"What I love about working with you ... "*

2 *"What I think you can do to increase your impact ... "*

3 *"A pattern that I observe that you may or may not be aware of is ... and the impact that has is ... "*

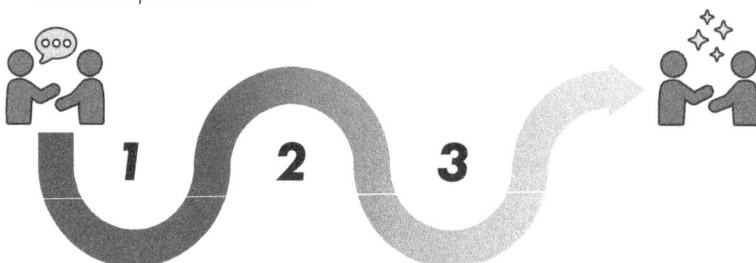

Expect them to respond, synthesize, and ideally restate. Thank them for responding. Show gratitude for the energy and effort it takes to commuincate honestly.

The day we received the aggregated results, we were all excited. The board, executive team, and entire organization were eager to see where we were exceeding goals and where we needed to improve. I received a call from Pete telling me that he and the chairman of the board wanted to discuss the results. They were both concerned that there were multiple comments that specifically named senior and executive team members and specific details that they were uncomfortable keeping in the document. I reminded them that we had committed to transparency and that team members would know if their comments were removed from the report. The chairman replied that it was not happening: "We are not sending this out with these comments." And that is what happened, regardless of the breakdown in trust it displays, or my leadership being compromised. Pete, although he could see both sides, deferred to the chairman because he was not given a choice. That was when I knew this would no longer be the place for me.

I decided to part ways with this company when their practices began to deviate too far from my values and did not deliver on their promises to move consciousness to a broader platform. I spoke with Pete and informed him of my intention to purchase the company back or leave. He shared the info with the board, who decided to put Little Sprouts on the market for other potential buyers. He shared that I could submit a bid if I was not an employee. I resigned so that I could structure a formal bid. By stepping down, I left millions of dollars on the table in employment contracts, equity, and bonuses. Sometimes staying in integrity to our higher self has a material cost. On June 25, 2012, Pete called to tell me AEG was selling Little Sprouts to another investment group. It was one of the most difficult moments in my life.

Although this situation was unfortunate at the time, it taught me quite a bit about the function of culture and how it truly is *what we do* versus *what we say we are going to do*. It taught me that consistency, structured practice, and cohesion are the bedrock of a culture—and that no matter how much training, money, or blood, sweat, and tears you place into an endeavor, it needs a healthy, deliberately developmental culture of courageous humans to thrive. Although every individual is the fractal expression of a culture, the culture itself is the sum creation of the people within it.

My colleague Pete used to use this Human Vibe expression about the two-way nature of the universe when we talked about leadership, "As above, so below."

Culture in SuperLoop Praxis

What does culture mean when it's being applied to organizations? How does a company culture form? Business leaders discuss it quite a bit but can rarely define and delineate it. What's your company culture? Did you deliberately design that culture, or did it happen to fall into place? Are you capable of judging whether your company culture is strong or weak?

Many professionals faced with this question would step back to their mission statement or a recitation of their organization's values. But those aren't really the whole of a culture. A culture is what we do again and again. As Dr. Stephen Covey often said during his fireside chats, "Effectiveness is the ability to get results while creating the environment to get those results again and again."[59] Effective cultures are focused on both results and the ability to sustain those results. Culture is not a one-hit wonder. It is not having a single good day on a team or hitting a few monthly KPIs. It is the ability to achieve those results again and again. It's the rules and expectations we set—and how we hold ourselves accountable to those commitments.

Culture is the water we swim in and the air we breathe. The secondary meaning of the word "culture" is an environment that is suitable for the growth of biological life, and this suits our conversa-

---

59   Stephen R. Covey, *The 7 Habits of Highly Effective People: Powerful Lessons in Personal Change* (New York: Free Press, 1989).

tion well. Every collective of people has, in one way or another, a culture. It's important to understand that an organization's culture is omnipresent; it's everywhere. It's the undercurrent and vibration surrounding your family, your business, or your organization.

Culture is also constantly being made and remade with actions and attitudes. What we practice eventually becomes our culture. Because of this, culture is not purely internal—rather, culture is shaped by a multitude of factors that are both expressions of culture and are also the factors that sustain it. Changing these pillars of culture can change the culture and changes in culture will change these pillars. This, essentially, means that changes in culture can quickly become positive feedback loops (self-sustaining cycles) that can strengthen or erode a culture rapidly.

Changing the available tools and material conditions surrounding a worker will not only make better work possible, but it will also increase morale. A change in morale, along with the change in material conditions, leads to a better expression of work—and the recognition that comes with a better output of work leads to more personal pride—which will increase possibility mindset—which is where the environment for maximized human potential and performance comes to life in culture. Influencing the conditions surrounding the cultural pillars quickly picks up momentum and leads to change.

We can understand this idea even further by breaking the culture into three modes it uses to convey information and create itself.

THE PILLARS OF A CULTURE

Culture is an amalgamation of factors. There are three broad pillars that influence culture and therefore have an enormous influence over how things are done at our companies and the results we receive from

PILLARS OF CULTURE

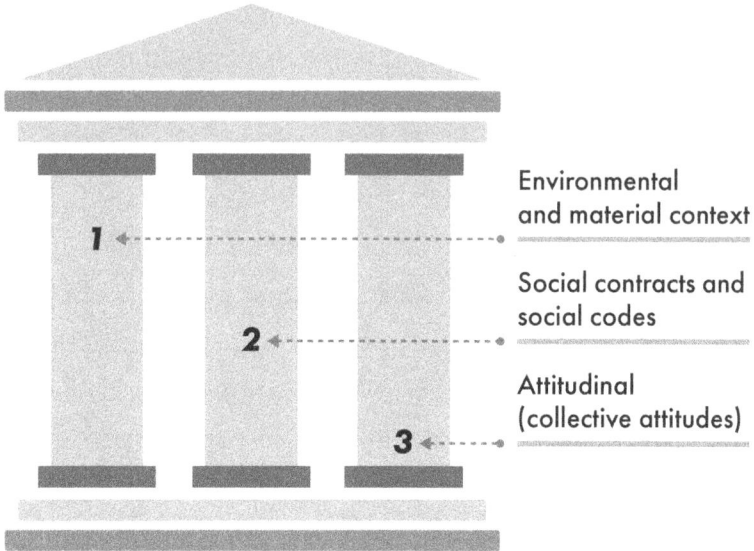

Environmental
and material context

1

Social contracts and
social codes

2

Attitudinal
(collective attitudes)

3

our workforce.[60] These pillars of culture, which will be explained in depth below, are:

1. Environmental and material context

2. Social contracts and social codes

3. Attitudinal (collective attitudes)

The first mode of cultural conveyance is the material aspects of daily life that possess a widely shared meaning to the people within the culture. In wider society, this includes movies, music, clothing, consumer goods, etc. Inside the culture of an organization, this refers to the products or services an organization creates, the internal materials it creates, and the physical setting in which the organization exists.

---

60   Brian L. Ott and Robert L. Mack, *Critical Media Studies: An Introduction*, 2nd ed.
     (Malden: Wiley-Blackwell, 2014).

Simply put, and echoing back to our chapter on the SuperLoop, the physical environment surrounding our organization is one of the core ways of creating our culture. Poor lighting, shoddy furniture, electronics that don't work, or cheap or nonexistent decor all contribute to the cultural sense of our organization. So, too, do music, aromatherapy, soundscapes, and scents. Promotional materials, art, organizational communications (including internal materials), marketing campaigns, language, and expressions of how we embody our mission create the culture of an organization.

A deliberately developmental organization will create artifacts that reflect their culture. The images, words, and messages in the material objects they create are absolutely critical. These ideas will also be extended to digital objects like websites, emails, and user interfaces. A company that cares about openness and accessibility should have attainable information reflective of these values. They have the opportunity to depict it in their artwork and content. A deliberately developmental organization would also want to have their values reflected in the distribution and accessibility of their cultural artifacts. Are your media artifacts captioned? Printed in multiple languages? Are they accessible to all employees or customers as is relevant? Is the language technical and/or industry speak, or does it make sense and is therefore valuable to all the users on the team creating true equity? When we see behaviors that do not align with our values, commitments, and strategic priorities, including KPIs and OKRs, do we handle them, excuse them, or ignore them?

The second pillar of culture is the social code (or rules) and agreements that guide a culture. The cultural artifacts will be made by the rules of the culture. The rules and social codes will determine quite a lot about how a given culture actually manifests in Operationalized behavior. Our social codes determine who we spend time with, how we value them hierarchically, and when and how we enforce rules. If we want to have a company culture of equity, our social codes and rules need to reflect that. Organizations should question how they can spread out the perks and privileges available to those in their culture if they have egalitarian intentions. Companies whose practices do not match their values will apply their rules and social codes in a fashion that contradicts their purposes and will not work in a way that is consistent with their long-term interests. Organizational hypocrisy, the disconnect between who we say we are and what we actually do, is one of the biggest factors in employee disenchantment.

The final pillar of culture is the attitudinal aspect. These are the shared ways of understanding the world within a given culture. In wider society, this might be reflected as attitudes toward the elderly or the young (Japan, for example, has a greater degree of reverence toward its elderly than the US tends to exhibit). It might be a culture's attitude toward education, art, or foreign policy. Within an organization, the attitudinal aspect is a measure of how the I/WE/ALL aspects of the company deal with concepts like hierarchy, privilege, fiscal attitudes, disruption, innovation, and a myriad of other critical concepts. Attitudinal dispositions aren't top-down; they're a collective evolution and expression of how individuals come together and make decisions. In many ways, it is the Unsaid of the organization. An organization's attitude toward a given idea or task can only be gradually cultivated with a genuine basis in practice.

An important thing to remember is that culture is ideological. Cultures determine what we privilege, what we limit, what we normalize, and what we encounter and internalize. This is why the element of peer-to-peer social learning within SuperLoop Praxis is so critical. *Culture is historical, which means it will always be influenced by what has happened in the past—which means the collective actions of the people within it will have a large, emergent influence on the creation of culture.* Every action matters in creating culture because it contributes to one of the core pillars of the culture. Culture is created by default or design. Each conversation, each behavior, each action item that does or does not happen creates the culture—and we ultimately get the culture we deserve.

When you're speaking, you're creating culture. When you're engaging in a practice, positive or negative, you're creating culture. When you are declining to engage (say, choosing to ignore behaviors in others that do not uphold commitments they have made), you're creating culture. *You are culture* in your presence and actions.

Being aware of these elements of culture means that we get to design our culture rather than inherit it by default. We get to consider our artifacts, our social codes and rules, and our collective attitudes. These are incredibly powerful opportunities to ignite transformation and Actionable Awareness throughout our organizations, families, communities, and our global humanity.

DESIGNING A CULTURAL SHIFT

In 2020, in the midst of the COVID-19 pandemic, G3 worked with a group of health and social service centers who engaged in one of the best cultural transformations I've ever guided in my career. When they first contracted G3 to aid in Operationalizing their values as a conscious company, they were in the midst of a leadership transition. Their initial concern was that they intended to engage in diversity, equity, and inclusion, but despite their values and intentions, these results simply were not actualizing as practices. With the advent of new leadership in the form of a prominent academic and lawyer who transitioned from deputy leadership and into the role of CEO, this group dedicated itself to growing its presence as a conscious company even further. For the sake of this analogy, we'll refer to this leader as Dr. Smith.

Dr. Smith had a long career of advocacy. He had already served as the regional head of a national civil rights organization for five years. He had also served on the board of trustees for multiple public health–related institutes and for higher education institutions. Dr. Smith had a long career and an exemplary body of work examining equity in healthcare and healthcare access.

Dr. Smith dove into transforming their organization according to SuperLoop Praxis immediately. He wanted to end the "legacy issues" that frequently plague company cultures that seemed so resistant to change. They knew that the organization existed in a state of Artificial Harmony, where certain conflicts in the company were not being addressed, and that this Artificial Harmony was manifesting as inefficiency and a loss of employee engagement. Those who felt they could not find the purpose and safety so critical to engagement were leaving or becoming less engaged and productive over time. This caused a gradual dilution of the values their organization was meant to represent. They wanted to ensure that the various communities, both patients and professionals, who made up the culture of the group felt valued and confident that their contributions mattered.

Dr. Smith had a number of goals that were culture driven. He wanted to use the strengths-based approach that G3 emphasizes in both hiring and employee development. The health institutes were the perfect partner for such a transformation. He recognized the realities of beliefs, biology, and behavior as influences on the I/WE/ALL and set about transforming the practices of the institutions with Authentic Communication, structured approaches to FeedForward, and Healthy Conflict.

Dr. Smith was also extremely effective and a cultural transformation agent because they undermined traditional notions of leadership and instead engaged with the notion of universal leadership espoused by SuperLoop Praxis—that anyone who influences is a leader. This resulted in giving a greater capacity for agency for the people who were being locked out of the previous culture. Dr. Smith Operationalized these changes with actual practices by adding multiple seats for patients on the board of this organization. Dr. Smith immediately accessed the opportunity for Innovative Capital through G3, securing hundreds of thousands of dollars to reinvest in the organization. They believed in the "nothing about us without us" principle and engaged his team at multiple levels in codesigning the operational development plan for the organization that would impart a greater sense of agency, rebuild trust, and increase engagement.

EQUITY AUDITS AND AN EMERGING STRATEGY

The Equity Audit process is unique to the Golden Goose Group, and it's a critical step in creating value in an inclusive culture. The Equity Audit involves G3 custom creating a series of interviews that are conducted across every level of a company. These interviews have several goals—using the Pillars of Culture, we create a landscape analysis to gauge the current company culture while identifying aspirational desires, thereby creating strategic and cultural goals for the future (or to renew the current goals).

Equity Audits are the first step an organization takes when it engages in the process of Operationalizing Consciousness. This is an exploratory, collaborative process that enables a SuperLoop facilitator to gather baseline data as a company begins its commitment to the work of transformation. This process is about diagnosing, with brutal (but egoless) honesty, What's Working and What's Not Working within a company. This level of candor and clarity creates an immediate transparency that allows a company's transformation to begin in a place of truth.

Equity Audits help cut to the core of ongoing problems in an institution. Eighty-five percent of the organizations I have worked with are practicing Artificial Harmony—they go along to get along. Similarly, they often have passive-aggressive cultures that create unsafe work environments by never addressing problems directly but creating all the stress of constant infighting.

Whether you're aware of it or not, if you are part of a team, you are engaging in one of these cycles. The Equity Audits are one-on-one interviews in combination with a brief organizational online assessment that enable a SuperLoop facilitator to engage in measuring the strengths and liabilities, qualitative and quantitative, in teams and, through extrapolation, the entire organization. It becomes the microcosm of the macrocosm.

Equity Audits explore the future, past, and present for transformational opportunities and ongoing challenges. The process reveals the unaddressed legacy issues in a company (what the SuperLoop system describes as Saying the Unsaid). These first steps are the initial sowing of change and innovation because the Equity Audit is the first place the concepts involved in SuperLoop are able to surpass the limiting beliefs they have about their own organization. The Equity Audit is where these new ways of being are introduced into the various levels of the company.

Dr. Smith's health and service organization undertook the Equity Audit process almost immediately after he took over as CEO. Dr. Smith's involvement and investment is one of the reasons this cultural transformation was so effective. The CEO was at the table, making this top-down initiative their priority rather than an agenda item that had no substantial investment from the leadership.

This involvement and investment made the Equity Audit process extremely effective. It revealed several factors that presented opportunities to be leveraged as part of the cultural transformation.

These points for development represent areas many companies and organizations invest in to strengthen their cultures and define their organizational identities:

The Equity Audit process revealed that one of the first steps this organization took in their evolution was to reform and recreate their affinity groups from a deliberately developmental perspective.

Affinity Groups

Affinity groups are organized meetings of like-minded individuals with common backgrounds, orientations, lifestyles, ethnicities, genders, or other identity-related traits that give them a shared life experience. These groups are beneficial in employee retention and engagement empowering employees to facilitate psychological safety by practicing inclusion and belonging. When properly implemented, they enable team members to have a safe space to show up while increasing the competencies learned in the art of listening and Authentic Communication courses. They can also prove beneficial in recruitment by demonstrating that a company has a commitment to ensuring employees' voices have a place at the table. Affinity groups can drive internal effectiveness by connecting different parts of the business and expanding internal understanding of each other's roles and contributions. On top of all these benefits, these groups also offer the opportunity to provide mentorship and development offering skills that lead to career advancement. They're effective culture resources that should be leveraged, but they, like any other element of a culture, also require planning and commitment.

This organization had already created a number of affinity groups, but, according to the Equity Audits, these groups were actually proving detrimental to the overall culture because they were not organized in a way that was not resulting in increased effectiveness. Without a solid process in place, the participants did not connect to the value and felt as if they were going through the motions. A study by McKinsey & Company revealed that individuals in ineffective affinity groups felt less included even than those in companies without affinity groups.[61] The Equity Audit revealed that individuals in the affinity groups at Dr. Smith's organization felt that the groups were unproductive and did not offer solutions or transformation. This is a common outcome in affinity groups that are not intentionally planned and executed. In my experience (and according to researchers for the USC School of Management and McKinsey & Company[62]), companies that desire to use affinity groups need to follow a few strategies in order to ensure that they are effective:

- Affinity groups need a clear purpose to prevent misalignment with the broader strategies of the company. The goals of the I/WE in the affinity group should be parsed and considered in the context of the ALL.

- Affinity groups need to provide detailed, deliberate communications to eliminate the disconnect between expectations

61 "Effective Employee Resource Groups Are Key to Inclusion at Work: Here's How to Get Them Right," McKinsey & Company, https://www.mckinsey.com/capabilities/people-and-organizational-performance/our-insights/effective-employee-resource-groups-are-key-to-inclusion-at-work-heres-how-to-get-them-right.

62 University of Southern California, "Employee Resource Groups," Center for Effective Organizations, accessed June 30, 2024, https://ceo.usc.edu/our-expertise/employee-resource-groups.

and reality. Explain the purpose of the affinity group from the outset. Respond to the communications and initiatives put forward by the affinity groups with clarity and directness. Utilizing all the communication tools this book has detailed—FeedForward, Connection Time, reflection time, Healthy Conflict, etc.—will empower individuals both inside and outside of the affinity group.

- Affinity groups must have a clear link between the organization and the affinity group.

- Affinity groups need training, materials, and mentorship on how to run an affinity group effectively.

Diversity, Equity, and Inclusion (DEI)

One of the other areas that the internal culture felt needed improvement was in the way in which this organization handled diversity, equity, and inclusion. In a theme that I see emerge frequently from Equity Audits, the employees and leadership in Dr. Smith's organization were tired of theoretical talk and historical data on racism that wasn't followed up with action. The employees wanted action, and Praxis that matched their values.

In my experience, "practice what we teach and preach" is the most critical component in creating integrity throughout the organization. If the members of a culture see that the values and rules of the culture are not reflected in action, they might sense duplicity, which is not what anyone signs up for. The inability to follow up declarations of values and philosophies with action eventually seems like it must denote hypocrisy or incompetence—and either of these is demoralizing to employees. If a company repeatedly proclaims the importance of diversity but then fails to ever follow that up by diversifying its workforce and its point of view, its employees will then see them as either unwilling or incapable.

The employees felt that the trainings on DEI were intimidating to those who were under-trained in those areas. This was a signal that DEI education was too infrequent and too surface level—it shouldn't be intimidating if the training is adequate; it should be empowering.

Employees also felt that DEI ideas were kept to those days of training and then went undiscussed and unpracticed in day-to-day operations. Perception is reality, and although these feelings toward Operationalizing DEI may or may not have been true, they became the collective attitude through which team members associated with the culture. Many employees completing the Equity Audit felt that the company-wide commitment to DEI was being undermined by the organization's unknown strategic priorities. A lack of clear, deliberate actions to enact values cannot happen if those values are not named, claimed, and aimed. Clarity creates buy-in—and the lack of it does the opposite, minimizing the opportunity for sustainable impact.

The implementation of affinity groups were aimed at addressing these concerns by finding actionable ways to address the values this institution held surrounding DEI while also signaling to the outside world that it was enacting the values it espoused. Dr. Smith and his team took the initiative to ensure there was more structure around the affinity groups to increase effectiveness and commitment. They were able to use the Actionable Awareness granted by their Equity Audit to make significant changes to their culture—and these changes gave the employees more opportunity to engage with their SuperLoop Praxis to turn what had previously been cultural difficulties into moments of engagement.

Transparency and Accountability

Another trend that frequently arises in Equity Audits is the lack of transparency when it comes to the internal financials of a company. The pay scales and benefits at these institutions were not as transparent as some of the team members desired. The apparent lack of transparency led to distrust among employees and to the spread of misinformation. This fostered feelings of inauthenticity among those who worked at the company because its operations didn't match the core values. Rather than being transparent, the management was using generalities and a lack of data statements when discussing particulars of positions and compensation. Transparency is critical to creating a deliberately developmental culture. Dr. Smith and his team made huge leaps in trust by handling this request to share data equitably and with urgency.

Mission, Values, and Strategy

Many of the leaders and employees at the Institution were unsure if they knew all of the organization's strategic priorities. A unified and directed culture must make these priorities clear across all divisions. The institutions wanted to empower people to discuss problems and challenges openly. A culture with a mechanism for expressing these ideas (a company that has Operationalized FeedForward, Clearing Conversations, and Healthy Conflict) will be able to cultivate a directed, deliberate culture. A culture that does not engage with its challenges and tensions will develop by default without the direction and input of the people it is meant to serve.

Dr. Smith moved to address all these points immediately. He required the entire executive team, including himself, to participate in educational sessions. This instinct alone signaled how dedicated Dr. Smith was to being part of the change he wished to see in the world.

Although having the C-suite at the table is standard practice for G3, it is one that we often have to spend considerable effort to convince people of. Many on the management and executive level would like to simply send their direct reports into training and have their company magically transformed. This isn't possible. Deconstructing and reconstructing at all levels is required for transforming systems. To paraphrase Dr. Gloria Steinem, "It's not what we learn, it's what we unlearn."[63] Unlearning and relearning need to occur at every level and cannot be an effort that is merely top-down or bottom-up.

So how do we know if our company culture is dysfunctional or failing because of a failure to engage with the SuperLoop? And how do we remake that culture from the individual SuperLoop on up through the I/WE/ALL?

DYSFUNCTIONAL AND FAILING COMPANY CULTURES

The path to creating a good culture involves the same factors as creating bad outcomes with culture. If the material artifacts (internal media, products, and promotion) we create don't align with our values and attitudes, our work and communication will also lack these values. If our social codes—the way we treat those inside of our organization and our customers—don't align with our values and strategic goals, we'll lose those values and goals. Failing in one area of our culture can lead to a cascade of failures in other areas because of the interconnected, continuous, and social nature of creating culture. There are a number of signs that a business culture is weakened or suffering.

---

63   Gloria Steinem, "A New Egalitarian Lifestyle," *New York Times*, 1971.
       The full quote reads, "The first problem for all of us, men and women, is not to learn, but to unlearn. We are filled with popular wisdom of several centuries just past, and we are terrified to give it up."

Businesses facing cultural challenges often indicate some or all of the following:

- **A lack of diversity and inclusion:** The current culture is not set up to take in new members that vary from the group that already makes it up. It privileges the existing views and identities without a curiosity that can lead to expansion and innovation. Cultures that lack diversity often overlook expertise and insight from unexpected sources. Diversity in thinking and experiences adds to the collective creativity.

- **Siloing:** The current culture suffers from a breakdown in Authentic Communication and collaboration. It is in a situation where portions of an organization are isolated from other sections that should be acting as partners or adjuncts to create systemic improvements. This usually occurs due to a breakdown in leadership that allows for a disintegration in communication, although that breakdown can occur at any level and does not only come from the traditional, top-down model.

- **A resistance to change:** The current culture doesn't have the tools to learn and to consistently socialize that learning. They cling to methods that don't work out of a desire to avoid confrontation and being uncomfortable. Often teams are fatigued with having new initiatives launched with much fanfare only to fizzle out when it is not prioritized and Operationalized effectively and collaboratively. These cultural issues are often described as "legacy issues" in the companies that I work with, and they are usually the result of some long-standing lack of perception, ignorance of the whole human, and complacency in the face of obvious problems. Our cultures are often hampered by our clinging to tradition just for the sake of tradition as well as the effort it takes to Operationalize new initiatives effectively. Flawed systems persist because it's easier to do what we have always been doing.

- **Fear of social and hierarchical consequences:** The fear of being vulnerable with team members prevents the forging of trust within a team. This lack of trust often comes from ego—it is difficult to admit to mistakes, identify weaknesses, or ask for help since these traits are not valued in cultures. This will manifest as dissatisfaction, a lack of retention, or disengagement and sabotage. Fear of conflict stems from a desire to preserve Artificial Harmony within the system where team members avoid difficult conversations and disagreements to maintain a false sense of cohesion.

- **Fear of material consequences:** Performance and fit will not necessarily be the metrics that allow someone to be retained in a culture with these traits, but advancement might instead be social.

- **A lack of whole human policies (often incorrectly described as work/life balance):** Companies that exploit the labor, time, or circumstances of their employees inevitably have challenges that are associated with the lack of support they provide for these employees. This lack of support will inevitably lead to individuals' personal lives impeding their work lives (they won't be able to maintain childcare, transportation, etc., as we described in the previous chapter).

These negative cultural situations inculcate themselves because they affect practices by activating SuperLoop responses, which in turn perpetuate more negative culture, which further affects practices. This is often why coming back from lunch five minutes late eventually becomes twenty minutes late. Practice feeds culture and culture feeds practice. The key to changing an ailing culture necessitates engaging with the multiple modes of innovation we've examined in the chapters leading up to this one.

CULTURE MAKES OR BREAKS OUR FUNCTION

The way that culture manifests on the I/WE level and then travels to the level of the ALL is explored in Patrick Lencioni's Five Dysfunctions model (as made famous in his *The Five Dysfunctions of a Team*).[64] Lencioni, as is clear from the title, describes this process in terms of what traits make teams unable to function—a result from the I/WE levels that spreads to the culture as a whole and potentially negatively affects the entire organization (the ALL).

Lencioni identified the following as the elements most likely to cause dysfunction on a team. For our purposes, these are the dysfunctions that are the most likely to cascade into the cultural traps we've already identified:

- Absence of trust

    - An absence of trust is encouraged inside of a traditional hierarchy. If a workforce is acting purely on a command/control basis and does not have agency, employees will feel as if they are powerless within the company culture. This leads them to not attempt any actions that require trust or transparency. Similarly, it will hamper their engagement with their peers and make socialized learning impossible.

---

64   Patrick M. Lencioni, *The Five Dysfunctions of a Team: A Leadership Fable* (San Francisco: Jossey-Bass, 2002).

- Fear of conflict

    - Teams that lack trust are unable to engage in Healthy Conflict surrounding important issues. As we've explored in our previous sections, the absence of Healthy Conflict will cause problems to fester and metastasize into larger problems for the organization. People *prefer* to avoid conflict because it's uncomfortable, because they fear consequences, or because their culture forbids it—this ultimately means that resolving the conflict is no longer a priority, and the ALL suffers as a result of said conflict.

- Lack of commitment

    - If teams are suffering from a lack of trust and from Artificial Harmony, individual team members will be unwilling to commit to decisions and follow through. This will result in an environment of ambiguity for the team that will radiate to a wider uncertainty within the ALL.

- Avoidance of accountability

    - The Artificial Harmony and conflict avoidance will result in an inability to hold individuals accountable for actions that hurt the WE. This inevitably means that problems spread from the I level all the way to the ALL.

- Inattention to results

    - According to Lencioni, all of the above factors will result in team members placing their individual needs (for career advancement, ego, or recognition) above those of the team (or their department/division). This inattention to team-oriented results ends up hurting the entire organization as deliverables are missed and other goals are forestalled.

CREATING A HEALTHY CULTURE

SuperLoop Praxis offers a transformative approach that emphasizes "antidotes" to common workplace challenges that come from poor cultural trends that have taken hold. These antidotes are behavioral and operational practices initiated at the individual and team levels (I/WE) with the aim to positively impact the broader organizational goals and values (the ALL).

Tenacious Trust is the opposite manifestation of the fear-based hierarchies that define traditional cultural power structures. Trust plays a pivotal role in this model, and this is trust that is centered around accountability, not on a moral or ethical assessment. In the SuperLoop Praxis, trust is the making and keeping of commitments. When we are able to steadfastly rely on the others in our organization to keep commitments, this trust forms the bedrock of effective teamwork. Trust is formed by consistently honoring commitments and communicating proactively when challenges arise and affect the WE/ALL.

Our culture is stable when we can trust those around us to do their job to the best of their ability and achieve the best results possible, and where others can count on us to do the same. A stable culture creates an environment where we all communicate consistently and openly when assistance is needed, when the deliverables will vary from what's expected, or when team members lack the tools to perform a task.

Netflix practices Tenacious Trust in their operations. Their corporate culture famously centers on "freedom and responsibility." Their employees are given substantial freedom in their roles, but this comes with high accountability. They, for example, allow employees to take as much holiday as they feel is appropriate without tracking it so long as they are upholding their deliverables. This approach relies heavily on the consistency and reliability of each team member to manage their workload effectively and report with transparency.[65]

Courageous Communication is another cultural practice that is closely linked to Tenacious Trust. Courageous Communication starts with introspection, questioning whether we are communicating bravely and taking responsibility for our actions. Individual accountability and Peer-to-Peer Accountability are critical elements of Courageous Communication. This practice requires that we set aside our conditioned behaviors that have trained us to always look good and project strength. Courageous Communication requires that we constantly poll ourselves to determine whether we are being honest with those around us by practicing transparency.

Tools like journaling, group reflective practices, and FeedForward are instrumental in developing the competencies for Courageous Communication. Fostering this kind of communication requires having the courage to confront difficult conversations and ensuring that each team member not only speaks but is also heard.

The culture at Microsoft shifted from a culture of competition to a culture of collaboration under the leadership of Satya Nadella. He created a culture of Courageous Communication by emphasizing practices where teams expressed both their ideas and their concerns freely—which meant that these teams were practicing a form of FeedForward across the company on the I/WE/ALL level. This also had the added bonus of creating a more inclusive environment with a diversity of ideas while also allowing for more innovation and less siloing.[66]

The practice of **Actionable Awareness**, as detailed in our earlier chapters, is all about conscious decision-making, taking into account

---

65   Netflix, "Culture," Netflix Jobs, accessed June 8, 2024, https://jobs.netflix.com/culture.

66   J. D. Meier, "Satya Helps Microsoft Rediscover Its Soul," JD Meier, accessed July 8, 2024, https://jdmeier.com/satya-helps-microsoft-rediscover-its-soul/.

our understanding of ourselves, our bodies, and the surrounding context. This awareness gives us the agency to act appropriately rather than being unconsciously driven by these factors. It's about recognizing our situations and asking, "Now that I'm aware of this, what will I do about it?"

Authentic Accountability involves embracing Healthy Conflict, seeking constructive feedback, and engaging in Clearing Conversations. It's a practice that emphasizes acknowledging personal responsibility in any situation. This concept challenges a culture to look inward first before attributing issues to external factors. It's a reminder that accountability is not about assigning blame but about taking responsibility for your contributions and building credibility and trust within the I/WE/ALL.

Companies who want to engage with the "antidotes" to poor culture need to be able to use conflict constructively (and to ensure that it doesn't become destructive). As we've discussed in the other chapters, this requires prioritization of a structured time and process— if individuals are looking to engage with their own accountability, it will enable the entire organization to use conflict as a growth point. Companies like Microsoft and Netflix can engage with freedom and productivity *because* they use conflict as an opportunity to refine their processes on the I/WE/ALL and to remove lingering issues.

Finally, organizations that want to create an effective culture must engage with creating **Regenerative Results**. Regenerative Results draw inspiration from Stephen Covey's insights on effectiveness. It's about achieving consistent results and creating the ability to achieve those results again and again. This reliability creates excellence and becomes the ethos of the organizational culture. This approach involves identifying areas of success for replication in areas that need improvement so that said high performance could be consistent across the organization. A practical example of this principle in action was seen at Greyston Bakery, where the marketing team initially focused more on nurturing relationships than on delivering quantifiable results. However, when they started providing concrete data by consistently measuring and assessing KPIs relating to work processes (quantitative; number of sellable products made hourly and qualitative; number of team members arriving before or on time), it paved the way for a more regenerative, results-driven model, emphasizing clarity, honesty, and authenticity.

A parallel example of this practice is the Japanese philosophy of Kaizen utilized by the Toyota Corporation. Kaizen acts as a continuous improvement philosophy that emphasizes that all employees should be collaboratively involved in identifying the most effective practices in their industry and to seek to both adopt and improve these practices. This creates a stronger culture that, in turn, is constantly seeking to better itself.[67]

All of these elements are critical to a healthy culture. In the companies that are lacking and potentially have flawed cultures, these elements will combine to create issues that radiate out from the individual. I have frequently observed challenges where a sales team leader failed to meet their targets and then did not communicate this challenge to the rest of their team. By the time this shortfall was discovered by the rest of the organization, it was so impactful it ended up costing the organization the ability to fund a position, which meant this lack of transparency led to layoffs inside of the organization. This was a breakdown of Tenacious Trust, on the level of the I/WE/ALL—the organization trusted individuals to engage in Courageous Communication and Authentic Accountability. When

---

67   Masaaki Imai, *Kaizen: The Key to Japan's Competitive Success* (New York: Random House Business Division, 1986).

neither occurred, it impacted the culture in a negative way that inevitably became a material consequence.

On the flip side, I've also worked with many organizations who have manifested all of these traits as Operationalized processes that led to a culture that achieved Regenerative Results as a natural extension of their healthy culture. In the example of the struggling sales associate, a healthy culture would have inbuilt support mechanisms for teams that need assistance to reach their targets—and where there are no repercussions for honestly communicating when they need help. This individual would have learned to seek support from the WE/ALL in a way that took accountability while providing FeedForward to others from whom she needed more support. These healthy cultures use data statements rather than vague, nonspecific comments. For instance, you would say, "You have been submitting your deliverables two to three days late the last two months and it has caused a drop in productivity for the team," instead of saying, "You never get your work completed on time." These specific statements allow for a state of Actionable Awareness that provides a clear path forward that is based on the current context.

The latter cultural model is obviously healthier on the I/WE/ALL level. Neglecting these issues leads to shortfalls in performance and organizational consequences. Addressing our problems with Tenacious Trust and Courageous Communication has no negative consequences beyond wrestling with our SuperLoop as we own our ego and fear and embrace our agency through accountability.

THE CULTURAL CONTINUUM

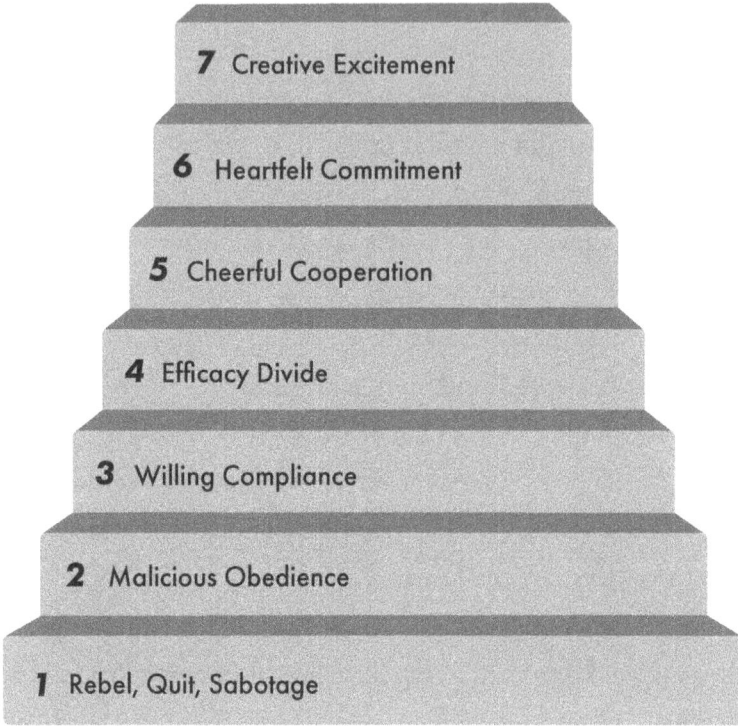

7 Creative Excitement

6 Heartfelt Commitment

5 Cheerful Cooperation

4 Efficacy Divide

3 Willing Compliance

2 Malicious Obedience

1 Rebel, Quit, Sabotage

The Cultural Continuum in SuperLoop, one of the core metrics in measuring the health of our culture by the commitment and efficacy we have in our work

HUMAN VIBE: "HOW WE DO ANYTHING IS HOW WE DO EVERYTHING." This Human Vibe is a mediation on the nature of anything with a large number of seemingly independent but actually interrelated parts. We tend to see our actions and opinions in one area as benign—

but when we contemplate our individual actions in reference to the cultural model, we see that our attitudes, the artifacts we create (the physical and informational objects), and the way we do or do not adhere to our values affect every other part of a culture. Our every action is ultimately meaningful and a contribution to the overall attitudes and outcomes. When we do something today, we are rehearsing for tomorrow.

"This Is What We Do Here"

An organization has reached cultural health when healthy actions become the default—when we engage with Tenacious Trust, Courageous Communication, Actionable Awareness, and Authentic Accountability and achieve Regenerative Results as a second nature.

This cultural shift that followed Dr. Smith taking the reins of leadership became very apparent to me as I was acting as a Vibe Guide for the organization and sat in on a Healthy Conflict session. It was deep in the COVID-19 pandemic, and Dr. Smith's organization had the opportunity to determine how their COVID-19 policy was going to be implemented since health workers were essential (and lifesaving!). During this period, it turned out that they had an employee who was unwilling to get vaccinated for religious reasons.

This became a subject of conflict for the leadership team in this organization. The old guard of the company wanted to fire this individual immediately. The younger leadership did not want to leave this employee in a poor situation because of their personal beliefs. Doing so would have been against the values of this company; after all, this employee had always served the organization well in the past and would be in serious financial trouble if they were to be dismissed.

This, in the past, would have become a point of conflict that might not have been able to be resolved. The two individuals spearheading each side of this debate were known to come to loggerheads easily, and neither of them were known to surrender. Before they went into a deeper conversation, they both requested support from coaches on the best approach and mindset.

They began with the first prompts in the Clearing Conversation, "My intention for this conversation is ... ," establishing the deeper root cause inclusive of their relationship, followed by, "What I take responsibility for is ..."

This gave them both the space to acknowledge they were gossiping about each other rather than communicating directly to solve the challenge. This cleared the way for a new conversation that ultimately connected both parties to the unified goal—to create a safe place, physically and psychologically, for their entire team.

They worked together to come up with a solution that suited both sides, honoring this employee's values while creating safety for the entire population internally and externally. Even more importantly, they modeled new behaviors for their teams. They acknowledged old patterns and stereotypes that were not serving anyone, and they aligned on a solution rather than staying polarized.

In the past, this was a conflict that would have partially been about leadership, seniority, "legacy issues," and the ideological underpinnings of getting or not getting a vaccine. With a system for Healthy Conflict and open communication in place, though, it became more than just an expression of individual opinions, it acted as a catalyst for discussions about the merits and practicalities surrounding the vaccination policy in a healthcare system during a pandemic. It became about the I/WE/ALL rather than just about the individuals having the conflict or solely the needs of the organization as a whole.

As the ancient wisdom goes, "The answer to the many is in the one." Each human in our sphere is valued as part of the whole collective that generates situations that can create solutions for all.

Dr. Smith's institutions were able to honor the individuals involved and to also ensure that the decision was made for the greater good while still acknowledging the individual and their identity.

If we consider our SuperLoop, its influence on the individual, and how that radiates out across the organization, we can create healthy cultures that are more productive and vibrant and continually striving toward Regenerative Results that make them stronger and stronger.

Dr. Smith and their leadership of this organization is one of my benchmarks for deftly using Actionable Awareness of the I/WE/ALL to achieve an incredible and sustainable transformation.

"If you want to go fast, go alone, but if you want to go far, go together."

—WIDELY USED PROVERB[68]

---

68   This is an untraceable saying potentially derived from the Luo proverb, "Alone a youth runs fast, with an elder slow—but together they go far." Despite commonly being identified as African, the origin is ultimately unclear, but the wisdom is indisputable. https://www.npr.org/sections/goatsandsoda/2016/07/30/487925796/it-takes-a-village-to-determine-the-origins-of-an-african-proverb.

"For every thousand hacking at the leaves
of evil, there is one striking at the root."

—HENRY DAVID THOREAU[69]

WE GET TO DO THIS

O ver the past almost forty-five years of my career, many moments have led me to have an overwhelming need to write this book: seeing Mr. George sitting in that tiny chair in the early days of Roxbury Community College's early education program, ready to change my outlook and set me off on a path of action with just a few words; seeing how leaders have engaged with SuperLoop Praxis to overcome issues that had been plaguing their organizations for so long they seemed baked into their DNA; experiencing the massive change the SuperLoop Praxis has brought to the companies that joined forces with Golden Goose Group and ultimately allowed their employees to embrace what it took to help the emperor find his clothes because they had the psychological safety and organizational support to do so.

Every time someone has called me, even years after we'd worked together, to tell me how different their lives were and how their entire

---

69   Henry David Thoreau, *Walden, Chapter 1* (Boston: Ticknor and Fields, 1854).

workflow had changed since they'd embraced the Praxis, it has reconnected me to the significance and imperativeness of this work. As Dr. King wrote, "All labor that uplifts humanity has dignity and importance and should be undertaken with painstaking excellence."[70]

But as I finish writing this text, the one that stands out to me is a recent one. I was working with the head of HR of a large multinational healthcare company to facilitate a transformation in their culture using SuperLoop Praxis. As we concluded our final meeting, she turned to me and said, "Susan, so where's the book? I want to tell everybody I meet about what we're doing here. You need a book, something I can go back to over and over."

And thus, the first impulse to write this book was born.

There is a great social and material need for us to find a way through the time we find ourselves in. We are in an era of dissatisfaction, disengagement, and mercenary attitudes that have divorced us from the grand goals that we can achieve as a collective.

We're in a time where there are many leaders who think that workers don't want to work, and a time when many workers think that leaders are only leading for themselves. We've all, on some level, lost perspective of the truly amazing things we could do because we've been conditioned by our dominant business culture to accept a limited view of ourselves and each other. This has had its cost. As I mentioned at the outset of the book, worker engagement has hit a twenty-year low, and the public discourse about work looks grim.

But the concepts we've discussed in this book, these methods of engaging with our humanity and bringing our whole selves into our work, are what will redeem us.

It's truly stunning to me how much can change in our lives if we live with an Actionable Awareness of what goes on inside and

---

70   Martin Luther King Jr., *Strength to Love* (New York: Harper and Row, 1963).

outside of us—of how we relate to ourselves, our teams, and our entire organization.

The methods in the book work because they're about knowing ourselves and then translating that knowledge into action. We are our beliefs, our biology, and our behavior—we are our SuperLoops. And knowing this means that we can finally interrogate our own perceptions and engage with why we have the reactions we have, why we are affected the way we are, and how we can understand others better with this new perspective.

I envision a future where everyone who picks up this book begins their quest by questioning their own assumptions about themselves and about their work. Where they begin to have curiosity in relation to perceptions about their limitations and their nature. Where they question and evolve their previous understanding of who they are and what their organization is. Changing your perceptions changes your reality.

I imagine a world where the leaders who read this book engage with the whole human inside their organizations. Where they create (or become) Pathmakers working constantly to develop, advance, and sustain all of their teams and employees and consequently have to deal less with hiring, onboarding, and turnover—where they are operating businesses full of committed humans who want to develop alongside their organization as they drive it forward. The I/WE/ALL are constantly reinforcing and sustaining one another and creating a more stable, healthy, and information-rich environment full of leaders who aid each other by Saying the Unsaid, engaging in Healthy Conflict, and practicing FeedForward that ensure we are communicating and collaborating in ways that our traditional business structures have simply not allowed for.

I want a world where leaders aren't the sole focus of attention, living and dying, based on the perception surrounding them. I want the substance of what they do to matter and for workers to have a clear link to the substance of what an organization accomplishes.

I know we are capable of being good people, running good businesses, doing good things. We do it all the time. Let's do it even better and remove all the old barriers that are holding us back; let's tear down those walls and build the roads that will make us into communities of practice that create a place for us to learn new ways of being and make us better humans. Let's build the paths that will make us better leaders, coworkers, community members, partners, public servants, and even better family members.

As the sentiments (and material facts) of our time are showing, these ideas, these human needs we have, are not something we can just ignore. We either engage with our SuperLoop in a deliberately developmental way or it engages with us, unplanned, spontaneous, and neglected.

As I wrote at the outset of this book, this isn't just a matter of life and death for organizations that are suffering through the current era; this isn't just something we *need to do.*

It's something we get to do.

SuperLoop Praxis is a huge opportunity, a chance for innovation and transformation.

The concepts in this book are concepts that you can work on by yourself. But one of the things you've likely taken away from reading this text is that—as strong and good as we humans are—we are even better when we are a team that can teach and lead each other.

If you want to take the next steps into pursuing this better future, please visit our site by scanning this code:

This is something that can change the world on some very fundamental levels and bring back some great ideas that we've let fall by the wayside. Let's make this new world—better yet, let's cocreate one.

As Rumi wrote, "Out beyond right-doing and wrong-doing there is a field. I'll meet you there."[71]

I'll see you there.

SUSAN LEGER FERRARO, MAY 2024

---

71   Rumi, *The Essential Rumi*, translated by Coleman Barks and John Moyne (New York: HarperCollins, 1996).

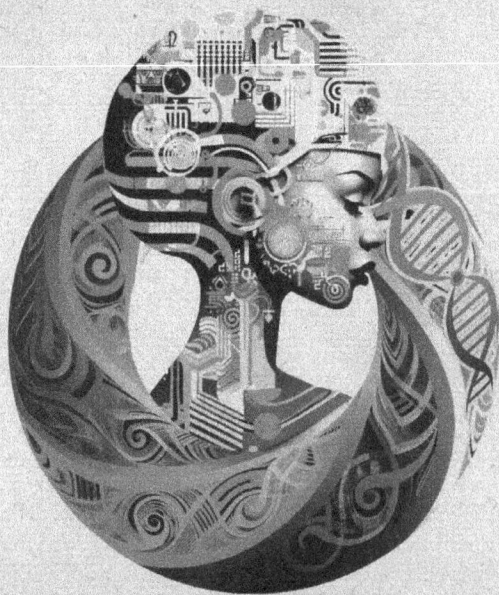

GLOSSARY

ARTIFICIAL HARMONY. The tendency humans have to maintain civility at all costs while ignoring other factors. It is a superficial sense of agreement or unity among team members that is not genuine or sustainable. Those practicing Artificial Harmony "go along to get along" rather than leaning into learning new ways to communicate. It typically comes from a fear of conflict and wanting to avoid difficult conversations. It tends to feed dysfunctional behaviors, whether passive-aggressive or overt, that allow ongoing issues to reach a boiling point and then become unignorable issues. Artificial Harmony is not sustainable in the long term and is tantamount to ignoring a dental cavity. It gets worse for the organization the longer it goes on as it prevents the team from addressing underlying problems and making the necessary changes to increase productivity. See page 101.

ACTIONABLE AWARENESS. The ability to be aware of the truth in ourselves and our environment and to act on that truth. This includes an awareness of our beliefs, our biology, and our behavior. Knowing about these factors at work in both ourselves and others enables a high level of awareness about the world around us—and an ability to act on that awareness. Without action, an awareness of issues with no committed action creates suffering. See page 77.

ACCOUNTABILITY. Reframed in G3 mindset, accountability means a shared responsibility for an outcome. If you are a part of the system, you are a part of the results. Accountability is making and keeping commitments within the I/WE/ALL. It starts with modeling Self-Accountability and expands into Peer-to-Peer Accountability and responsibility for all through the overall vision, mission, values, and strategic goals of the organization. See page 231.

AUTHENTIC COMMUNICATION. Involves being open and honest and making data statements with your communication. It involves dispelling Artificial Harmony and engaging with others with the I/WE/and ALL in mind. Authentic Communication uses the Curious Question and Call Forward models. It is a mutually beneficial process with the foundations of Generous Listening that fosters the ability to be in integrity with oneself while creating the space for others to show up authentically. When a relationship is in "breakdown," where one or more persons have broken their commitments, it requires taking responsibility by having a Clearing Conversation and renegotiating how you will move forward in a way that meets the needs of all involved. See page 66.

CALL FORWARD. The process of engaging with an individual directly with the belief that their commitment is to be the highest and best version of themselves aligned with their commitment to the team's values and in a neutral fashion, this creates the space for us all to show up in new ways rather than perpetuating labels based on past patterns of behavior. It is the foundation of Peer-to-Peer Accountability, as we are collectively responsible for holding each other accountable to the written, verbal, or implied commitments made for maximum team efficacy. See page 109.

CLEARING CONVERSATIONS. A process for using Respond-Ability, Healthy Conflict, and Curious Questions to acknowledge breakdowns in agreements, real or perceived, and renegotiate expectations and commitments while reaching alignment for moving forward with the relationship(s) to clear the Unsaid and create unity in achieving results. See page 149.

CULTURE. Patterns of behavior we have normalized. See page 205.

CURIOUS QUESTIONS. A tool that is used to set the foundation for Generous Listening. An individual utilizing Curious Questions will have an awareness of their biases going into communication. Curious Questions utilize authentic curiosity that creates a space for deeper listening. As soon as you sense yourself going into judgment, you practice giving the benefit of the doubt ("I am clearly missing something here. I get to practice Generous Listening by using Curious Questions"). Curious Questions are collaborative instead of demanding a desired response. Curious Questions are invitations to communicate that support all parties in being seen, felt, and heard. They are distinctly about the lack of judgement, starting with the person asking the Curious Questions. See page 109.

EFFECTIVE CULTURES. The ability to get results while creating the environment to get those results again and again. See page 212.

EQUITY AUDIT. The process of creating a quantitative and qualitative evaluation of the culture and operations of an organization. The Equity Audit is a means for an organization to engage with Actionable Awareness of the state of their culture and operations—and to create a plan for education, development, and transformation based on that awareness. This process involves interviews, observation, informational reviews, and assessments across an organization and at every employment level. See page 217.

FEEDFORWARD. The process of providing insight for members of your organization using a defined framework that uses data statements and prioritizes both psychological safety and results/action plans for the future. It is how we practice building the competency of Authentic Communication by acknowledging the value a person brings while also building our collective capacity to acknowledge where they can improve and where there are blind spots. See page 38.

HEALTHY CONFLICT. Non-ego-driven conflict conducted within an environment of psychological safety. It has specific parameters and does not involve a power differential as a source of domination. It is seeking to work out opposing ideas within a team/organization. See page 108.

HUMAN VIBE. The truisms, cultural distillations, and codes of thought espoused by G3 and SuperLoop Praxis. They encapsulate important lessons about Actionable Awareness and our relationship to our SuperLoop. Human Vibes can often be immediately understood on their first read/reception and set the foundation for behaviors within cultures. See page 13.

I/WE/ALL. The three levels G3 uses to categorize an organization. The I level is the level of the individual. The WE level is the team/division level. The ALL level is the entirety of the organization and the cultural identity of the organization. These levels are in a state of constant interaction and influence, so most ideas and practices should be examined from each of these perspectives as part of our planning and execution to ensure comprehensive levels of impact. See page 41.

INCLUSIVE HIRING. Hiring that engages with competencies (abilities) rather than on the basis of the traditional metrics used in hiring (degrees, in-industry experience, etc.). It is more inclusive than traditional hiring because it avoids focusing solely on the arenas from which system-impacted people are marginalized. See page 57.

PEER-TO-PEER ACCOUNTABILITY. A system where individuals in an organization rely on their peers for encouragement, course correction, Call Forwards, and Healthy Conflict. This differs from the traditional top-down model, where accountability comes only from hierarchical positions. The peer-to-peer model is more resilient (a lack of oversight from one leadership position comes from a limited number of people who can be fallible and have a limited bandwidth) and creates Authentic Leadership rather than authoritarian leadership cultures. See page 40.

PRAXIS. When practices manifest our values and ideologies in the world as literal action. Praxis is when a practice embodies our values and our intentions in the world. Feeding the hungry would be engaging in Praxis for a humanitarian. SuperLoop Praxis involves using Actionable Awareness of the world and agency in the self to create a better life and do better work to fuel that life. See page 5.

RESPONDABILITY. The ability to respond (to plan and use Actionable Awareness about the self and one's environment) rather than to react (giving in to the immediate SuperLoop-driven impulse). See page 16.

SAYING THE UNSAID. The process of recognizing the unaddressed subtext that is present in most social interactions. Saying the Unsaid allows for stronger conflict resolution, more transparency, and the ability to be part of the solutions rather than commiserating about the problems. See page 83.

SOCIALIZED LEARNING. A model that intentionally designed that creates focused growth by continually challenging, evolving and reflecting on individual and collective results. See page 8.

SUPERLOOP. A self-reinforcing cycle of our beliefs, biology, and behavior. Our beliefs impact our body chemistry, which influences our thoughts. These thoughts influence our behavior, and those behaviors reignite the cycles by influencing the beliefs. Our SuperLoop can be a compass for navigating our world by paying attention to these three domains and understanding why they are activated, or it can be an uncontrolled force in our lives that constantly influences our actions. We use our SuperLoop or our SuperLoop uses us. See page 5.

SUPERLOOP PRAXIS. The system of practices for engaging with, managing, and maximizing the opportunities presented by the SuperLoop. It allows for an Actionable Awareness of our consciousness, bodies, and environment so that we can harness these factors rather than be dominated by them. See page 5.

SYSTEM-IMPACTED INDIVIDUALS. People who have been impacted by systemic racism, sexism, economic deprivation, generational poverty, educational exclusion, or other systems that underpin society. These individuals face greater challenges when trying to access wealth and other forms of well-being. See page 25.

VIBE GUIDE. An individual who is responsible for interpreting the social and organizational context in a meeting, project, or gathering. This individual acts as an active aid to engaging with SuperLoop Praxis as an organization enacts a transformation. See page 76.

Ta-da!

Printed in the USA
CPSIA information can be obtained
at www.ICGtesting.com
JSHW020828290924
70575JS00028B/138/J

9 798891 882188